BORN
ANXIOUS

BORN
ANXIOUS

The Lifelong Impact of Early Life
Adversity—And How to Break the Cycle

DANIEL P. KEATING

St. Martin's Press 𝄞 New York

BORN ANXIOUS. Copyright 2017 by Daniel P. Keating. All rights reserved.
Printed in the United States of America. For information, address
St. Martin's Press, 175 Fifth Avenue, New York, N.Y. 10010.

www.stmartins.com

The Library of Congress Cataloging-in-Publication Data is available
upon request.

ISBN 978-1-250-07504-8 (hardcover)
ISBN 978-1-4668-8648-3 (e-book)

Our books may be purchased in bulk for promotional, educational,
or business use. Please contact your local bookseller or the Macmillan
Corporate and Premium Sales Department at 1-800-221-7945, extension
5442, or by e-mail at MacmillanSpecialMarkets@macmillan.com.

First Edition: April 2017

10 9 8 7 6 5 4 3 2 1

To my clan, whose love and support
is the foundation for this book

CONTENTS

AUTHOR'S NOTE

The names and identifying characteristics of some persons described in this book have been changed.

PROLOGUE

A NEW LIFE BEGINS. AT the start, complex changes are taking place, as a single cell grows in just a few months' time into a thriving fetus. When all goes well, with the fetus developing in the protected space of the mother's womb, a healthy baby soon emerges. Parenting then takes over to help the baby develop into a healthy child.

Alas, sadly, sometimes all does not go well. Toxic substances may get past the protections surrounding the womb and either terminate the pregnancy or make this new life especially challenging. Or, harmful genetic variations can have the same result. And sometimes, hidden from view and not understood until quite recently, a biological change of a different sort may be made while the fetus is still in the womb. Whether that change is made will be determined by the *stress level of the mother*.

Of course, expectant moms do have things to be stressed about. They want their children to grow strong and healthy, and pregnancy can often be a difficult time physically and emotionally. So let me be clear that we are not talking about everyday stress. But if an expectant mother experiences unusual levels of stress, this hidden biological change can happen. This can be triggered by extreme situations like an abusive relationship, exposure to violence, or job loss. But this same change can also be triggered by more common concerns like divorce, conflicts at work, or even excessive concerns about being able to help her baby find a place in an increasingly competitive world. If an expectant mother is experiencing high levels of stress—for whatever reasons over a period of time—her elevated stress levels may, through a mechanism we are just coming to understand, result in her child being "born anxious."

We also know that this biological switch can flip even *after* the child is born, if the primary caregiver is under enough high-level stress to get in the way of providing that child with the necessary nurturing. Once again, this baby will show signs of having been born particularly "anxious."

As babies, children like this can't be easily soothed. As young children, they struggle to get along in school or with friends because they react badly to even minor bumps in the road. As teenagers, they may long for peer connections but retreat from social life because it seems so overwhelming, as they are driven to scan everyday environments looking for potential threats. As adults, their behavior is off-putting to coworkers, family, and friends because it is so unpredictable, and they themselves find it difficult as they have little trust that their well-being will matter to others. Though early life stress is not the only possible cause of these behaviors, it is a major one, the impact of which has been overlooked until recently. And it can affect anyone, at any level of social class.

Anxious people live their entire lives with a heightened sensitivity to their environment, worried about missing signals that might warn of danger or threat. This heightened sensitivity, leading to feeling perpetually anxious, agitated, stressed-out, and overwhelmed, is hard to endure day after day. More recently, we've also learned how heavy a toll this anxiety can take on their physical health. As early as the midtwenties, they can feel shrouded in a general malaise; in midlife, they are prone to heart disease; and eventually they may live shortened lives.

But here is something we haven't focused on enough. This "anxious, high stress" burden is carried not only by those who are directly affected but also by those who are close to them. Figuring out how to deal with someone whose hair-trigger response is hard to predict, and how to help them to regulate their emotions and behavior, can prove ineffective—and exhausting. Furthermore, as we've recently learned, stress is contagious, so those who might otherwise be able to provide support are likely to be feeling quite stressed themselves.

The stress epidemic in modern society is showing up as increases in stress-related illnesses, and in people's increasing reports of feeling anxious, agitated, and overwhelmed. Advertisements bombard us with promotions of supplements that claim to reduce stress, though evidence of their effectiveness and safety is weak or nonexistent. There are surely a myriad of reasons for this stress epidemic, but research has now shown us the links between early life stress and a lifetime of being stressed-out, the health and developmental effects of that kind of life, and the stress epidemic in society that can, in turn, increase the odds of early life adversity in the next generation.

To figure out how to actually break this cycle, we need to

understand how it really works. We'll need to look at this from several perspectives, using a number of tools from different scientific disciplines. What is the nature of the hidden biology that launches a lifetime of challenges for health and development? How can we recognize the pattern of constantly being stressed-out, in ourselves and others, and what can we do about it? How can we buffer our children against this?

And perhaps most important, why is this happening now in our society, and can we do anything about that? In the United States, and many other modern, wealthy countries, the core answer, as we will see, is rising inequality, affecting the poorest to the richest and everyone in between. This thoroughly modern stressor is less visible than the threats to survival of our shared past from predators, violence, or deprivation, but is often just as lethal. What we will also see is that there are ways to break the cycle in our own homes, workplaces, and communities—but first we need to understand how it truly works.

INTRODUCTION

THE SUMMER AFTER I TURNED fifteen, I helped out at a literacy program in one of the most economically distressed neighborhoods in my home town, Baltimore. There I met and tutored a boy named Jason. I came to know Jason pretty well. Indeed, I have never forgotten him, for he awakened in me the feeling of déjà vu.

Jason wanted to learn. He tried his best to grasp what I was trying to teach, although without much success. It seemed as if the process of learning, more than the material itself, eluded him. I had no idea how to break through to help him.

But Jason stood out in my mind for another reason. He was prone to outbursts. They came on suddenly, like a summer storm. When they occurred, he'd angrily lash out at another child or even at one of the counselors. Other days, instead of lashing out, he'd withdraw so completely that he'd refuse to acknowledge anyone.

That summer, I heard over and over again from the adults

around us about what it meant to grow up like Jason, in a tough neighborhood, deprived of opportunity. I'm sure they told us that to make sure that kids like me were never uncharitable toward kids like him. But I stayed quiet whenever this explanation was offered. And I knew why. Because of a boy named David.

David had been my classmate at the parochial elementary school we both attended. One day, when I was a fourth-grader, I was asked to take charge of our boisterous class a few afternoons a week. (I know this sounds strange, but back then our parochial school, like many others at the time, was overcrowded and understaffed.) Before I took over the class, I would have described David as a kid like me. He came from the same kind of suburban, middle-class, education-oriented family. He seemed to be a pretty good student. It was only when I took charge that I began to notice the ways in which David stood out. Most obviously, he switched without warning from friendly and easygoing to angry and out of control. His outbursts were often triggered by something as innocuous as a small change in what we were working on in the class. And once unraveled, he took a long time to calm down.

I had no idea how to handle David. To be honest, he frightened most of my classmates and me with his temper. And I noticed how hard it was for him to stay focused on the schoolwork that the teacher had given the class to work on.

I lost touch with both Jason and David over the years, but I never stopped thinking about them, because every once in a while, when I was doing tutoring or leading a Scout troop in college, I ran across another kid just like them. When I did, I wondered what had happened in their lives to make them the way they were. I sensed that no person could live his life at such a fevered pitch without exhausting himself, not to mention sabotaging himself when it came to schoolwork, friendships, and just day-to-day-life chores. Why couldn't these kids see that as well and just get control of themselves? Although I didn't know it then, the pattern of behavior I was trying to understand did not occur only with boys. It often plays out a bit differently in girls, but the underlying patterns are the same.

Not surprisingly, when it came time to pick a college major, I was irresistibly drawn to psychology and went on to earn a PhD in developmental psychology—which aims to understand the many influences that shape our lives. While others struggled to figure out the intellectual question they wanted to spend their lives studying, I already knew mine. I was going to try to figure out the Jasons and Davids of the world.

I started with the fact that kids like them manifested three observable characteristics: they couldn't sit still in a classroom, couldn't concentrate, and couldn't control their emotions or their attention. It was easy to rush to the conclusion that these issues sprang from some very real intellectual deficit that made learning frustrating and painful. In other words, if they found learning easier and less draining, they'd calm down.

Yet some of these same kids were clearly smart by most measures. They could understand and talk about ideas, often with considerable maturity and insight, even though you wouldn't know that from looking at their school records. And most of them manifested the same volatility in the school yard that they did in the classroom. What they all shared, I kept feeling, was not some common intellectual or learning deficit but something that drove them off the rails at critical moments, in unpredictable ways.

Kids like me, I began to believe, rarely experienced these kinds of derailments, and that allowed us to deal with life's frustrations without getting waylaid on the path to success, while kids like Jason and David somehow always did.

Over time, as I read the research of colleagues and began to do some of my own, I developed ever greater empathy for all the Davids and Jasons. Nothing went smoothly for them—not school, not social relationships, not work. Late at night, after going through mounds of data, I began to wonder if some cruel evolutionary sorting process was going on. Kids like me seemed almost destined to *thrive* in life—and to do so with assurance. Kids like David and Jason seemed destined to *struggle* through life. It was still just a notion: I didn't yet have the research to back it up, but I couldn't set it aside. The unfairness of it haunted me.

Fast-forward some twenty years to the early 1990s. Mountains of research on child development and the building blocks of learning and thinking, including my own, still had not yielded one good, comprehensive explanation. Nor had the millions of dollars spent on early childhood education and school reform substantially closed the academic gap between what I continued to think of as *strugglers* and *thrivers*. I knew the answer couldn't be just economic: some kids in very poor neighborhoods thrived and some kids from middle-class, upper-middle-class, and even wealthy families struggled. We could not predict with any real success which kids would fall into which category. Nor did we understand why. All we knew was that something was going on that was beyond the control of schools and teachers and that it couldn't fully resolve itself even with early childhood intervention.

Indeed, something was going on. But as this book will explain, research by our network led me to believe that this something, alas, had altered the Davids and Jasons of the world long before they started school—indeed, possibly as early as the womb or no later than the first year of life. That's why in many cases early educational programs were not as effective as we had hoped. They, and many others, carry a hidden burden that has gotten into their very biology—affecting, as we will see, the way that they encounter and deal with stress and anxiety every day of their lives. My hope in writing this book is that as knowledge of the problem becomes disseminated, we will better understand the source of their struggles and how to break the cycle that holds them back. Because there are helpful actions parents, schools, and society can take. There are actions that kids like David and Jason can take, to help them control and even prevent the derailments, giving them the same chance to thrive that kids without this burden have had. There is even the possibility that if this help is offered early enough, and under the right conditions, what began as a disadvantage can be turned into an advantage, and kids like David and Jason can mature into some of the strongest candidates for positions of leadership in society.

But first we had to fully unravel the mystery of what exactly was holding these kids back. What was happening in the womb or the first year of life that controlled this sorting process?

.   .   .

Someone once said that success is the child of luck and determination. In our case, the determination came naturally: my research teams and I had put in decades of hard work. But we needed that little bit of luck to make it pay off. Fortunately it finally came knocking. I was presented with a rare opportunity to approach the problem from a much broader perspective.

In 1992 I was approached by the Canadian Institute for Advanced Research, a Canadian-based think tank that funds multidisciplinary research on complex problems. CIFAR asked me to put together a research network of senior scientists to explore the origins of why some adults are healthy and others are not, and why some children succeed and others don't. This question emerged out of new research, especially a famous study of British civil servants that showed one group suffering more illness and early death, compared to another group working in the same section of London—despite similar working conditions and universal health care. What was the difference between the two groups? The healthier—and longer-lived—group was of higher social status in the civil service. The pattern was clear—but why was it happening?

In later chapters I will explain exactly how we came to understand that a key triggering mechanism was indeed responsible for both patterns: childhood strugglers were more prone to medical problems—back pain as young adults, early heart disease as they grew older, and many other conditions. This susceptibility showed up in different ways in different individuals. Some of these differences were linked to gender, and some were associated with race or ethnicity. But what was common, as we discovered, was that early life stress was a key launching pad for both childhood struggling and adult health problems. What continued to elude us, however, was the mechanism by which these two sets of sortings were related.

As our group—which initially included investigators from psychology, psychiatry, epidemiology, neuroscience, and primatology—began to probe this more deeply, it became more and more obvious that this "something" was powerful and widespread in its effects. It was also astonishingly durable over the human lifespan, affecting individuals well into adulthood and even old age. So we had to look for something that had found a way to "get under the skin" of strugglers from the very start of their lives, to biologically embed itself in their very nature.

Together with colleagues in epidemiology and primatology, among others, we first considered and quickly rejected a bad-gene explanation. Genetic vulnerabilities are real, but they manifest themselves in breakdowns in specific functions—Down syndrome affecting cognitive development, for example—not, as we were seeing, negative effects crossing behavior, psychology, health, and longevity.

We also considered the possibility that we were dealing with some environmental contaminant such as lead, which as we know is a major poison affecting brain development in children (and the reason why the people of Flint, Michigan, are so justifiably furious with their government for allowing it to leach into their drinking water). But again, lead and other toxins typically wreak damage on specific organs and bodily systems, not across the board and not with such wide-ranging impacts on both mind and body.

Finally, we also explored two suspect but popular notions, variously labeled "bad parenting" or "bad culture." A pileup of serious economic and social risks certainly increases the chances that a child will struggle developmentally, but as a full explanation for children like Jason and David, it had some key flaws. Most important were the emerging findings from studies of resilience—children who had experienced significant adversity in early life but thrived nonetheless. And many kids with apparent advantages in life, at least on the surface, were clearly struggling with life's challenges. Beyond the scientific limitations, the pure nature (genetics) and pure nurture (environment) accounts suffered from another serious drawback: both struck me as fatalistic in many ways and were problems we couldn't really solve.

The triggering mechanism, as we discovered by putting together findings from many corners of the scientific enterprise, involved *a biological change made in response to an adverse social experience in very early life that altered the ability of that person to deal with stress.* How we came to that conclusion is the focus of the next chapter, but an introduction to this recently identified biological mechanism sets the stage for understanding how important it is.

By 2001, we had been working on this puzzle for almost a decade, and in 1999 had already published a joint volume (*Developmental Health and the Wealth of Nations*) laying out the key elements of our story to that point. In that year, we invited as a guest presenter for our group a researcher named Michael Meaney. He and his team had been searching for the causes of hyperactive stress responses in rodents that had suffered poor nurturing just after birth—an animal model of early life adversity. That pattern—poor early nurturing leading to stress dysregulation (for convenience, let's call this SDR)—had been found in a number of animal behavior labs around the world, and when followed into later life, these animals revealed problems in behavior and health that looked like what we were seeing in the human findings. But what Meaney and his colleagues at McGill University discovered led to a new field called social epigenetics.

Let's take a moment to put this in context—to see how dramatic these findings were to us and why they transformed how we look at the differences between struggling and thriving, and between who's healthy and who isn't as adults. The science of epigenetics rests on a simple idea, though one that is complex in its many details. (And again, we'll take a closer look at this in Chapter 1.) The basic idea starts with the realization that the human genome—our genes—carries all the essential information for making us as individuals. Genes determine what cells to build, what they should do, where in our body they should go. Genes are designed to produce and release a wide range of biochemicals for specialized purposes—the overall term for this is "gene expression."

But there's another, lesser-known actor than the famous human genome—the *epigenome*. This includes numerous mechanisms that can change how the genes work—that is, how the genes are expressed. These are changes brought about by things that happen *after* the DNA instructions are laid down at conception. Some of these are "housekeeping" changes that happen immediately after conception, to halt or activate the expression of specific genes. Other changes—known collectively as "epigenetic modifications"—are responses to physical substances that can happen at any point in life. The link from tobacco to cancer, for example, appears to work partly through epigenetic changes.

But what Meaney's group found went beyond that: *social experiences*—in this case, low maternal nurturing in early life—could also cause epigenetic changes, altering how a given gene carries out its designated task. The specific change they first found was in a gene that is central to how the stress response system works (NR3C1, which plays a key role in what is known as the "glucocorticoid feedback loop"). The details do matter, and we'll come back to them in Chapter 1, but here's the gist. An epigenetic change known as "methylation"—named after methyl, the chemical compound that is responsible—shuts down a key gene that is designed to tell the stress system to turn off when a threat has passed. The result: stress dysregulation (SDR) that leads to an oversupply of the stress hormone cortisol on a pretty constant basis.

This was indeed the missing puzzle piece that made sense of our findings from biology to child development to societal patterns in health and development. We now understood the mechanism responsible as well as the conditions under which this mechanism works. The difference in the children who struggled was indeed biologically induced. A gene meant to turn the stress response system on and off in the presence or absence of a threat had been locked on, making it difficult for the stress system to stand down.

The children whom we had categorized as "destined to struggle," the ones who saw threats everywhere and whose inability to control their emotions and attention seemed to be standing in the way of their achieving all sorts of important life goals, were in fact expressing the childhood characteristics of SDR. Adults who have this dysregulated stress response usually know who they are and so do we. These are the people who seem to experience stress constantly, often way out of proportion to the problems they face. This can be expressed in many ways: anxiety, agitation, anger, distress, distraction, or withdrawal—and often more than one at any given time. Not all cases of struggling are caused by early life adversity and SDR of course—there are real genetic vulnerabilities, exposures to toxic substances, trauma, and accidents, to name a few. But we found that the link from early adversity to later life problems ran through social epigenetics and SDR, accounting for much of the struggling we saw in the population.

No matter who we are, no matter our age or place in society, we are all destined to experience moments when stress takes over our lives. Evolution intends us to do so in response to life's tragedies and dangers—violence, threats, deprivation, loss—and to experience the heart-pounding nervousness that accompanies any life-or-death decision. Without the ability to activate our stress response in times of crisis, we would likely not have survived as a species, because it is the very strain of stress that focuses our attention and supplies a burst of energy when a lion is hiding in the bush or starvation is imminent—the kind of terror-filled problems our ancestors faced repeatedly.

What we experience as stress is the well-known fight-or-flight response, the sense that we must act or our very lives could be in danger. It is a built-in adaptive response and an essential key to our survival.

All of us, throughout our lifetimes, will experience these moments of fight or flight, but usually only when confronted with a fairly substantial threat to our lives or our dignity. Indeed, part of growing up is learning to separate fake threats from real ones and learning how to stay calm enough to make the distinction. Individuals carrying the burden of SDR not only have difficulty separating real threats from garden-variety scuffles and annoyances; they can get worked up into fight-or-flight mode by almost anything that is unexpected. And not just worked up with a twinge here and a pang there. Before they know it, they are sweating profusely, their chest is tightening, their pulse is racing, they feel flushed, and they may even faint if it is too overwhelming. Once this happens, all they can focus on is how to shut down this heart-pounding stress.

The need to find release from this overpowering anxiety and tension is all-absorbing. Many do so by lashing out at others or throwing a fit. Now consider the following: In childhood and adolescence, those without this elevated stress response are becoming more and more adept at learning how to read the actions of others. Thus they learn how to reserve this do-or-die response for very special real threats because they can stay calm long enough to see that most of these threats peter out on their own. But those who suffer with SDR feel they can't take the chance to wait and evaluate because something deep inside is telling them to act, not consider. So as one group gets more and more adept at flicking off annoyances, distractions, and even the inappropriate behavior of others in order to concentrate on the task at hand, the other is becoming more and more incapacitated.

A common denominator among the baby who cannot be soothed or who falls asleep only to awaken in a panic twenty minutes later, the toddler who can't stop having tantrums, the child in school with hair-trigger aggression who cannot sit still or concentrate, the adolescent who retreats from a threatening world, and the adult with an elevated stress response is this dysregulated stress system. A key gene that is meant to release cortisol in the face of danger and stop releasing cortisol when the all-clear signal is sent is no longer able to shut down the stress response because it is responding to a message from early in life: eternal vigilance is the only thing that will keep you alive.

Imagine yourself as a child trying to concentrate on learning basic subtraction while something deep inside you is whispering in your ear, *Stop, look around—there is danger somewhere.* No surprise that you're fidgeting and can't sit still. No surprise that you're unable to concentrate. No surprise that you're itching to run.

Imagine you're on a swing and a kid playfully twists the rope, but you feel in your bones that he's dangerous. A voice in your head says, *He's out to get me if I don't scare him off.* No surprise that you turn on him.

Imagine night after night when you can't sleep or suffer nightmares because you feel like there's a tiger in the closet.

Every morning you wake up agitated, snarling back at that tiger.

A kindly teacher wants to know what is troubling you, why you always seem to fuss, but you can't answer her because you can't articulate the feeling inside you. All you know is that you feel worked up. You can't explain why you throw fits in the classroom. You wish you could control them. You don't seem to be able to catch on to the schoolwork the way the other kids do. You wish you were like them. You wish you weren't you.

Is it any wonder that a child living with the constant message *Watch out, never let your guard down, trust no one*, and who is experiencing these inexplicable pulls on his emotions can often grow into an adult who eventually turns to alcohol, drugs, and food to relieve the immediate symptoms of excess stress? When well-intentioned observers urge them to relax and smell the roses, they think, *If only it were that easy. If only I knew how.*

This degree of stress not only affects the lives of the strugglers—those who are stress-dysregulated. It can initiate a vicious cycle that affects all of us. Imagine that you are the child who playfully twists the swing. Suddenly you are being screamed at and then knocked to the ground. The other kids are laughing at you. You are angry, even humiliated, and you go home and attack your younger brother. Your parents can't understand where all this anger is coming from. Frankly, neither can you.

Imagine that you are an adult with an overbearing boss who turns every little problem into a catastrophic event. Your mistake, he tells you one morning, is going to take down the whole organization. Intellectually you know he is exaggerating, that he is always catastrophizing. But human nature being what it is, you can't help but get upset. Even if your stress regulation system is working just fine, it's hard to entirely dial back the anger you feel before heading home. And so the stress seeps into your family. The reality is, stress is contagious at the biological level.

In fact, the more of us who carry the burden of SDR, the more the rest of us get worked up as well, even at times appearing to be stress-dysregulated ourselves. We are not, but we sure act like it. The notion of a stress epidemic in American society is gaining traction for a good reason. Many of us see evidence of it every day of our lives. To address this, we need to understand how it works at its core.

If you are reading this introduction, no doubt you are wondering to whom SDR happens and why? Are you yourself stress-dysregulated? Does it explain your husband or your father or your daughter? Those of you who have taken a few courses in biology probably remember that traits that no longer serve our survival tend to get weeded out—this is why we have such a large amount of "junk DNA," genes that are no longer expressed in humans. Surely this relentless stress isn't good for any of us. So why did it survive?

One way to think of the epigenome is that it's a tool by which evolution enables the species to survive. The decision by the epigenome to lock that stress gene—in effect, to remove its control over the on-off switch—is made in response to one question asked while a child is still in the womb or in the first year of life: what kind of world will this child be entering—one that is kind and supportive or one that is harsh and unforgiving? If the latter, the best way to ensure that child's survival long enough to allow him to reproduce—and reproduction is the only thing evolution really cares about—is to make sure that he never lets down his guard, even as a child, never forgets that danger is just around the corner.

For our ancestors this made perfect sense. And today you can bet that this gene is locked in most children born in war zones— as some recent findings from conflict zones in the Congo confirm. That makes sense. We know that children born during even short periods of famine or deprivation show evidence of this welding. Even more worrisome, there is increasing evidence that this epigenetic change in the stress response system can be passed down to later generations—an epigenetic inheritance, with no changes to the DNA.

Here in the United States, one of the wealthiest countries in the world, we are seeing a stress epidemic, which is showing up in people's health and sense of well-being. Not all of this can be attributed to the biological embedding from epigenetic changes—any of us can be affected if the external stressors are strong enough—but surely a substantial part is. Why is this happening? Partly because, as we noted above, this epigenetic change can be passed on from generation to generation. But the single most important factor creating this society-wide stress is rising inequality.

A woman who fears that she or her husband will get laid off may be hyperstressed during her pregnancy. But rising inequality affects a broad swath of people who currently fear a dramatic fall in class status, for themselves or for their children. The first woman wonders how she will provide for her child in the immediate circumstance; the second worries that her child will fall out of the middle or upper class altogether, with dramatically diminished life chances.

In either case, when the concerns pile up and her worrying gets severe enough, her cortisol levels can get high enough to pass into the blood of the fetus. It's this excess flood of stress hormone—cortisol—that locks the stress gene. And if the child from either family feels its basic needs for food, comfort, and affection are not being consistently met, or if that child senses an inner tension or stress in his or her caregiver, this same biological change can occur during the first year of life.

Of course, rising inequality is far from the only reason why a pregnant mother or her infant might unintentionally signal a fear of the future to the epigenome. Single parenthood, a feckless husband, divorce, job insecurity, ambivalence about being a parent, rising housing prices, market crashes, illness, racism, crime—there's a long list of situations that can drive up cortisol levels. Rising inequality is not the cause of all early life stress, but it often amplifies the effects.

"Stress is killing me"—you've probably uttered that phrase at some time in your life. But for those who experience chronic high levels of stress, this phrase is sadly on the mark. We're learning now that stress *is* a silent killer, one that affects our very biology, and those of our families and others around us. Further, it's one that targets us during a particularly vulnerable window—from our time in utero through the first year of our lives—with implications that reverberate for the rest of our lives. It's a haunting story, to be sure.

This book tells the important story of how stress in early life can fundamentally alter the life of a child, making it harder for him or her to learn, make friends, find a life partner, earn a living, and keep healthy. It includes important information about what expectant and new parents can do to minimize stress and thus avoid exposing their children to a lifetime of chronic stress. Further, it includes thoughts—and evidence-based information—about what we as a society can and must do to reallocate resources to help parents during this critical period. And it urges all of us to acknowledge that the elevated stress system of others is not just their problem but ours, to solve together. We have the potential to break this vicious cycle—in individual lives and families, but also in society.

1

EARLY LIFE STRESS:

The Biological Impact of Rising Inequality

THE BATTLE OVER NATURE VERSUS nurture—over the importance of qualities we inherit as a result of genetics versus those that come from things we are exposed to after we are conceived—has raged for more than a century. And at the time I entered the field of psychology, that battle had entered a particularly nasty phase. Little did anyone know that a new science was taking shape that would forever transform this battle—in fact, it would render it obsolete. The result would directly impact my chosen field.

In the late 1980s and early 1990s, headlines like "Murders Surge As Crack Spreads" and "Race, Genes and IQ" screamed from newsstands. The social safety net was rapidly fraying, with proposals to roll back the Great Society emanating from the White House. The liberal efforts of the 1960s were widely viewed as having failed, and even if this wasn't entirely accurate, the political direction seemed to be taking a different tack. Doubts about the costs of social programs, their effectiveness, and even their fairness were rising fast.

From this swell of anxiety and uncertainty emerged the outspoken University of Chicago political scientist Charles Murray, who argued that welfare and the social safety net had done little more than encourage dependency. Murray launched a project designed to test the idea that racial inequality was based on, as he put, "intractable race differences" in intelligence. With *The Bell Curve*, the bestselling book he coauthored with Harvard psychology professor Richard Herrnstein, hit the bookstores in 1994, Murray would push this stance even further, claiming that African Americans and the poor could not succeed because "what's holding them back is that they're not bright enough," and that welfare along with remedial education efforts should be tossed overboard. "For many people, there is nothing they can learn that will repay the cost of teaching," was his dire conclusion (*New York Times,* October 9, 1994, "Daring Research or 'Social Science Pornography'?"). The book took a clear stance on the nature-nurture debate, and it spawned a rancorous public debate, with other scholars attacking the credibility of its statistical analyses, its unstated assumptions, and its failure to consider alternative explanations.

Nurture wouldn't go down without a fight, though. Taking an opposite tack, but with equally dire implications, the "culture of poverty" arguments began to make a comeback to redirect blame away from ineffective antipoverty programs and place it on those who were the most vulnerable. Harking back to Daniel Patrick Moynihan's famous and controversial 1969 report, "The Negro Family: The Case for National Action," there was a resurgent belief that the ills of the "underclass" arose from cultural deficiencies. In *Code of the Street,* the sociologist Elijah Anderson argued more persuasively that the claim of presumed deficiencies misunderstood the real cultural imperatives at work. Because inner-city youth were blocked from more traditional ways to succeed and achieve a meaningful identity, the violence and criminality that they engaged in were in fact adaptive in their circumstances—even if they ran against mainstream norms.

In part, both of these schools of thought rose in reaction to the claims of the Great Society and War on Poverty initiatives, which implied—or said outright—that increased attention and funding would soon take care of persistent problems by improving the social environment. But with rising rates of violent crime and limited progress on child poverty, clearly they hadn't succeeded in the public eye. The argument that more spending was the answer, that we hadn't done nearly enough to implement promising programs like Head Start, was met with increasing skepticism, even when there was evidence to support this unpopular rebuttal.

So we basically had a replay of the nineteenth century, when the social Darwinist belief in the survival of the fittest—as shown in the "natural superiority" of white Europeans—led directly to the eugenics movement in the early twentieth century. This supremacy of the nature view resonated clearly in the work of Murray and others, like the psychologist Arthur Jensen, who explained the better performance of whites in the United States by claiming that they had a superior genetic endowment. And yet the counterargument—that genes played no role and that good nurturing could conquer all—wasn't viable either, as we uncovered genetic vulnerabilities that created particular challenges for some children—like dyslexia, attention disorders, and other learning disabilities.

This nature-nurture game had been going on for so long, and so fiercely, it almost required picking a team—Team Nature or Team Nurture—not only among culture critics, but among researchers as well. Even those who acknowledged that both nature and nurture mattered couldn't move the ball much—no one could say exactly how they mattered or what to do about it.

Meanwhile, these extreme positions exerted powerful influences on key policy decisions that were being made based on faulty science—sharp reductions in education for low-income populations, deep cuts in the social safety net, "superpredator" laws that removed judicial discretion in favor of harsh mandatory sentencing—all of which created consequences that bedevil us to this day, like mass incarceration, which rose dramatically over twenty years, from an already shockingly high rate in 1990 (1,860 out of every 100,000) to over 2,200 in 2010—and almost twice that for African American men. The statistics alone fail to capture the disruption created in individual lives, families, and entire communities. Although most striking for African Americans, the pattern was similar for white Americans, as the overall rate of imprisonment continued to rise, long after the drop in the violent-crime rate that began in the mid-1990s and still continues.

In short, we were stuck. We were stuck in policy debates based on stubbornly misguided science. Researchers, including me, were stuck in the middle of an either-or dichotomy that was increasingly sterile. And we were all stuck in a nature-nurture debate that had gone nowhere for more than a century.

DISRUPTION: A NEW APPROACH

In the spring of 1992, out of the blue, I got a call from someone asking if I might have time to speak with a man named Fraser Mustard. I had no reason to suspect that this call would not only change my research career dramatically but also lead to a new way of looking at nature and nurture, eventually breaking us out of the box we'd been mired in for decades—and in the process offering insights that would affect not just the debate on poverty but other social ills, including chronic stress, social inequality, health and health care, and mortality.

I'd heard the name before—I knew his team had played a significant role in the discovery that aspirin could help to prevent heart attacks and strokes. As I soon learned, Fraser Mustard was nothing if not ambitious in his goals. Just like the work leading to the now-common use of low-dose aspirin to prevent initial or subsequent heart attacks that have extended the lives of thousands, he was deeply interested in new areas of science that could make a difference for society as a whole. Quite soon, this man with the unusual name would come to mean much more to me, drawing me into the heated nature-nurture dispute in an entirely unexpected way, leading me to a completely new way of looking at why some kids struggle while others thrive.

.   .   .

A decade earlier, Mustard had founded the Canadian Institute for Advanced Research, an international think tank that was driven by the simple insight that the best way to tackle really complex problems with multiple causes was to assemble a diverse team of the very best experts capable of addressing each cause. With very little by way of introduction, and no explanation of why he was calling, Mustard asked me if I'd heard about three recent studies that, he said in his probing way, had intriguing implications individually and perhaps even more intriguing implications when considered together.

He started by talking about something called the Whitehall Study. This now-famous study of the health of British civil service employees in the Whitehall district of London, led by British epidemiologist Michael Marmot, was conducted twice, once in the 1960s and again starting in the late 1980s. Marmot found that lower-ranking employees were four times as likely to suffer serious illness (such as heart disease, chronic lung problems, and depression) and earlier deaths than higher-level administrators. Interestingly, because researchers had narrowed their observation to these British civil servants, they were able to exempt the usual reasons offered to explain such a phenomenon: the physical demands of a job (pushing paper is, after all, not arduous labor), limited access to health care (there is universal health care in England) and lifestyle (smoking, diet, and exercise), which they measured through questionnaires filled out by participants. And yet, even with these factors removed from the equation, between 65 percent and 75 percent of the health differences associated with social status were left unexplained. This mystery caught Fraser's interest—what else could be causing those lower on the totem pole to fall ill? But he was also taken by the fact that these weren't the usual victims either. Until this point, research had been centered on the health impacts of being poor, but here, the sufferers were clerks in the British civil service. They were lower on the pecking order, to be sure—but they were hardly poverty-stricken.

Fraser then moved on to the work of an American psychologist named Emmy Werner, who focused on resilience—the reality that some children who experience early life adversity, indexed by various risk factors like economic or social disadvantages, nevertheless enjoy substantial success in later life. She had recently published a book, *Overcoming the Odds*: *High Risk Children from Birth to Adulthood,* which followed a group of 505 men and women on the Hawaiian island of Kauai—many of whom didn't graduate from high school and went on to work as unskilled laborers—and tracked risk and stress as it played out in their lives. Ultimately, Werner found that those who were able to rebound from setbacks and troubles in early life had benefitted from a close nurturing relationship in childhood or adolescence—either with a parent or with someone who stepped in to fill that role. This success against the odds set by early life adversity was not a widespread phenomenon—it benefitted around 10 percent of those she'd followed—but it suggested an intriguing possibility: that the right kind of nurturing might repeal some of the damage low social status could inflict.

Lastly, Mustard brought up a theory put forward by the British medical researcher David Barker suggesting that a baby's nourishment in utero was a crucial factor in predicting aspects of adult health decades later, including blood pressure and heart disease. This so-called Barker hypothesis, which had emerged two years earlier, in 1990, represented a revolution in the way we thought about how social factors impact adult health. Until this work appeared, most of the focus was on stressors that happened during adulthood, like difficult working conditions. This research showed that the more important link was between prenatal conditions in utero and later adult health. Barker had examined the detailed medical records of 449 men and women born in Preston, England, between 1935 and 1943, following them from birth until their late forties and early fifties. Those most likely to suffer heart disease were the group whose birth weight was substantially less than expected based on placental weight—indicating the fetus had not grown to optimum weight. Although Barker made the link between fetal growth and adult heart disease clear, he did not offer the cause.

After reeling these three studies off, rat-a-tat-tat, Mustard now paused for breath. And then: did I see the connection? He could see from Marmot's study that there was clearly something else—something linked to our socioeconomic circumstances—affecting our health that had not yet been revealed. Werner's work on resilience offered the glimpse of a solution, or at least a way to ease the harm our early life circumstances might inflict on us. And yet Barker raised the disquieting possibility that there might be factors, in addition to the social elements Marmot had introduced, influencing our health before we'd even entered the world.

What was really at the heart of these seemingly disparate studies, however, was the notion that one could not simply point a finger at nature or nurture. These findings were beacons signaling that there was something larger and more complicated going on than the intellectual leaders of our day would have us believe. Mustard didn't yet know what that something was, but it seemed clear that venturing further down this road might offer an alternative argument to the sterile debate raging around us.

I was intrigued. My own work to that point had focused on trying to find the hidden forces driving otherwise bright kids—the Jasons and Davids of the world—to lose control when push came to shove in the classroom or at home. And I, too, had been working to escape the confines of the national conversation. In speaking with Mustard, I saw that by closely studying the interplay between the two—nature and nurture—we might uncover just how they influence our lives. And perhaps this would offer real help for those whose fates were being inexplicably altered by their circumstances *and* their genes.

Within days, Mustard and I were meeting in his CIFAR office in Toronto. (I was working as a professor of applied cognitive science at the University of Toronto at the time.) When I encountered him in person, I glimpsed the U of T football player he'd been long ago—he was a towering figure with a sturdy build. And yet his white ring of hair, like a halo around his otherwise bald head, combined with his frank open-mindedness, made him seem more like a Benedictine abbot from the tenth century.

He got right to the point: he wanted to launch a new CIFAR program that would examine the developmental reasons behind why some people remain healthy while others do not. He had an instinct that the research we'd discussed was only the beginning of a larger conversation. Clearly, the classic accounts for the ways in which social status—whether measured as income, school achievement, or career standing—affected our health were not enough. He wanted to find the missing piece. He also believed that more than just our cardiovascular health could be determined in our early lives. Barker's work may have only opened a door. In the end, it boiled down to this question: what else could be radically affecting the health of certain adults— and when did it take hold?

MAKING THE CONNECTIONS

A year later, we launched a new program—the Human Development Program (HDP)—with me at the helm. We assembled a diverse group of experts, which included an epidemiologist, a couple of neuroscientists, a child psychiatrist, two developmental psychologists, and a primatologist, who worked with monkeys exploring the behavioral and physiological consequences of early nurturing deprivation. The studies that Mustard had cited—by Marmot, Werner, and Barker—were like three pieces of a puzzle, offering an early, albeit incomplete, picture, and now we had to fill in the rest.

We decided to start at the beginning—that is, the beginning of life. We would seek out research expanding on Barker's theory that our experience in utero affected our adult health. Barker's work had been very specific, looking mainly at heart disease; we wanted to explore other problems that might have their origins in utero. And we also wanted to follow through on how environment might continue to affect a person after birth.

Soon, the two epidemiologists on our team found a way to delve into this. They had been working with data from a govern-

ment study called the 1958 UK Birth Cohort, which followed
the lives of 17,000 people born in England, Scotland, and Wales
over the course of a single week in 1958. Researchers had tracked
these people from birth forward—checking back in on them at
ages seven, eleven, sixteen, twenty-three, and thirty-three (they
would carry on from there, but at that time, participants were in
their thirties). At each meeting, our colleagues presented new
analyses of participants' health, education, career, and general
life circumstances. They quickly discovered that individuals' socioeconomic standing at the time of birth correlated with a wide
range of difficulties throughout life: lack of success in school,
delinquency, low career achievement, and health problems. This
bolstered and, more importantly, broadened the work done by
Marmot and Barker: socioeconomic circumstances at birth had
an impact throughout life. And the consequent problems were
as sweeping as academic difficulty at the age of eleven or general
health at age thirty.

In addition, we discovered that this was true across the classes;
socioeconomic status had what we called a "gradient effect," another way of saying that these health and behavioral consequences
were strongest at the lowest end of the scale. They continued
to play out, though with decreasing impact, all the way through
the middle and upper classes. Not surprisingly, children born
into families with the lowest socioeconomic status (SES) struggled academically at the start of school and continued to struggle
academically. But just as in Marmot's Whitehall studies, this
pattern was repeated at each higher level of SES—children at
each level performed worse than those at the next higher level,
right to the top.

Still, SES was basically a stand-in for what we were truly looking for, which was the factor—the *why*—leading to these debilitating changes that were taking place early on and unfurling over a lifetime. We still did not know why social status would cause a teenager to falter in school or a forty-year-old man to have a heart attack. Given that we had an inkling from Barker that whatever was happening could occur even in utero, it seemed there was something that was "getting under the skin" or, as we came to describe it, becoming biologically embedded. But what could this mystery mechanism be?

FALLING INTO PLACE

Monkeys, as it turned out, would offer us our first clue. One of our members, Stephen Suomi, a primatologist and scientist at the National Institutes of Health (NIH), had been studying the effect of early adversity on rhesus macaques, a species of Old World monkey. Several of his studies involved housing a small group of newborn monkeys together without an adult in order to see what would happen in the absence of nurturing. Sure enough, after a year, when Steve put these monkeys back with the larger troop, they experienced an array of challenges, from behavioral struggles to addiction.

I recall watching a video that Steve showed us of one of these "peer-reared" monkeys roughhousing with another monkey. At first, it seemed like normal horseplay, but it soon became apparent that the troubled monkey didn't know when to stop. He continued to pummel his friend, even after that friend had curled

up into a ball, his head in his hands. In fact, no amount of signaling came through—not lying on the ground, not trying to walk
away. The troubled monkey just kept right on hitting.

It was around this time that we first began to see a link with
stress. A number of studies had shown that the level of the stress
hormone cortisol could be reduced by nurturing as simple as
mere physical contact. One experiment discovered this by accident: simply picking up rats from their cages in a lab in order
to perform research inadvertently reduced their cortisol activity. Guessing that cortisol might be at the root of the monkeys'
behavior, Steve tested them for the opposite problem: a rise in
cortisol that he thought might have resulted from their harsh
upbringing.

In a series of studies, newborn monkeys were grouped together and supplied with ample food but with no adult monkey mothers. Sure enough, his peer-reared monkeys had an
amped-up stress response system: their hypothalamic-pituitary-
adrenal (HPA) axis, the system that controls the release of the
fight-or-flight hormone, was in overdrive. It activated with less
provocation and kept going long after others would stand down.
When Steve presented us with his findings, the glint in his eye
revealed what we also quickly grasped: the link from hyper-
HPA activity to these monkeys' hyperaggression and inability
to control their own behavior was a breakthrough discovery. It gave us our first hint as to what might be going on in
humans—what was getting under the skin—early on and generating difficulties throughout life.

Steve then presented us with a second important finding:
when offered the choice of water, juice, or a cocktail of juice

and alcohol, the deprived monkeys were far more likely to choose the alcoholic drink. And they were *far more likely to become addicted*. Although Steve warned us not to look at the monkeys as directly related to humans, the parallels in the data were striking—addiction was one of the key factors associated with high stress reactivity in humans. We felt strongly we were on the right path.

Not long after Steve had discussed his illuminating research with us, the psychologist Megan Gunnar, who came to give a guest lecture at CIFAR (and soon afterward joined our network), provided us with the next crucial piece of the puzzle. She was in the early days of what would become a landmark multidecade study of the lives of a group of orphans who'd grown up under devastating circumstances. In the 1980s, Nicolae Ceauşescu, the Romanian dictator, had concluded (incorrectly, alas) that his country required large-scale population growth for economic health. As a result, people were prohibited from using birth control. While all large-scale policies have unintended consequences, in this case they were particularly brutal—a vast number of unplanned children wound up in Dickensian orphanages, warehoused in large rooms with row upon row of cribs, and only a small group of adults to supervise them. These caretakers had little time for—and weren't expected to give—even the most basic human contact. These orphanages were basically run as if they were factories with an assembly line of babies to be perfunctorily changed and fed.

Soon after this tragedy came to light, with the collapse of Ceauşescu's regime, a significant number of these children were adopted into well-off families in Europe and the United States, where Megan and other researchers had begun to study their development. The findings were striking: virtually all of the children who were not taken into adoptive homes *before the age of one* showed the same patterns that the monkeys had shown, from a dysregulated stress response system to difficulty forming relationships.

The dramatic effects of deficient nurturing in Steve's and Megan's research, in both monkeys and children, clearly showed its unquestionable impact on the stress system and on problem behavior later on. And so we now decided to focus our attention on stress, both on how it is shaped by experience and how it changes behavior and health.

Enter Michael Meaney, a professor at McGill University who specialized in neurology, stress, maternal care, and gene expression. Like Suomi, he had been studying animals displaying SDR, but he was working with rodents rather than monkeys. Michael, too, had discovered similar physiological differences and behavioral problems in rats who'd been deprived of maternal nurturing—specifically, the "arched-back licking and grooming" of the newborn pup—but he also arrived with a brand-new and as yet unpublished finding. He had actually found a biological mechanism—a process that seemed to explain why those who experienced stress early in life had so much trouble thereafter. As he explained what he had learned, we suddenly realized that this was the missing piece of our puzzle.

Meaney's lab had been studying the link from deficiencies in early nurturing to SDR for some time and had been seeking the underlying biology of *why* this happened. As Michael recounted the story, a chance meeting at a conference with a McGill colleague, Moshe Szyf, provided the inspiration. Szyf, a pioneer in the growing field of epigenetics, hearing about the work of Michael's group, suggested that an epigenetic change to genes that control the stress system might be worth exploring. Up to this point, nearly all the work on epigenetics had looked at it in terms of normal fetal development—where it plays a major role in controlling how and when genes work— or in response to physical inputs throughout life, like the effects of smoking as it leads to cancer. The spark here was to explore whether *social experiences*—in this case, early nurturing— could have a similar effect.

Ordinarily, our stress response system amps up or powers down proportionate to threats we face. If there's a lion about to pounce, or a man with a gun walking our way, the system releases cortisol, which puts us on high alert. When the threat passes, the cortisol is shut off. Well, it turned out that when Michael's newborn rats experienced the stress of poor or missing maternal nurturance at a high enough level, something happened that prevented the cortisol from being shut off.

This process is what's known as an epigenetic change: a gene's function is altered—either switched on or switched off—by an external factor. In this case, the external factor was extreme childhood stress without comfort, and it caused an epigenetic change called "stress methylation." Methylation means that a methyl group—a specific type of chemical molecule—has attached itself to the on-off switch that is a part of every gene. In the particular case of stress methylation, the gene whose job it is to tell the HPA axis to stand down—to shut off the flow of cortisol—is silenced. High levels of stress experienced in early life can methylate the key gene that controls this stress system. When this happens, we live as if constantly facing the pouncing lion or the man with the gun.

There it is, I thought, *there's our answer: stress can get under the skin, changing the very way our genes function.* I was far from alone in recognizing how this changed the landscape of how to look at early life stress. As my colleague, Clyde Hertzman, who had a penchant for pithy and pointed conclusions, remarked on first hearing about this new social epigenetic story of the biological embedding of SDR in early life: "It's a way of getting a message to a newborn that it's a dangerous world out there, so you'd better live hard, live fast, and, very probably, die young."

The minute we learned of this epigenetic effect we realized the potential implication for understanding not just people at the lower end of social status, but all of us. Clearly, it fit with the social-inequality story we had been pursuing for a decade. Low socioeconomic status as a marker of early life adversity, with the lifelong consequences we had come to understand, was a natural fit for this new story. But it went well beyond that. Difficulties in early nurturing arise from many other sources than economic and social disadvantage. In the modern world, the stresses of managing dual careers or the worries about the hypercompetitive world that one's children may face can interfere with the kind of nurturing that infants need. At a later point, we learned that this epigenetic change could follow another social pathway: If the mother is hyperstressed during pregnancy, the same stress methylation can follow. Parents from lower SES groups may have a greater risk of stressful pregnancies or stressed-out early parenting, but it can happen at any level of SES—which was entirely consistent with our findings on how stress can show up at any level of society: it can happen to anyone.

Our team was not alone in grasping the profound implications of this dramatic new science; soon researchers around the world joined this exploration, revolutionizing the way we look at child development. Starting immediately after the publication of several seminal papers by Meaney's group in the early 2000s, we have seen a massive undertaking to extend and understand the social epigenetics of early life adversity. And from all we've learned, what we know about early adversity altering our genetic functioning is likely to at least double in the next few years. For now, however, we can say with certainty that stress can change the way our genes work, with consequences across the lifespan. And beyond. It turns out that this epigenetic change—which doesn't affect the DNA at all—can be passed down to the next generation; this has been found in animal studies, but there is recent evidence that it happens to us, too. This remarkable finding means that the social experience of early adversity can make a change that becomes part of our biology—and part of our biological inheritance: *nurture becoming nature.*

Once this was clear, I began to give talks—to psychologists, teachers, social workers, community health groups, bankers (who were helping to fund CIFAR), legislators, and policy makers, essentially anyone whose own work would be enriched by this remarkable news. Naturally, everyone also had a personal interest; inevitably, there were many questions to answer with respect to their own families and their concerns about the effect this was having on our society at large. How much stress is too much? What does stress methylation look like? What can I do if it seems that I or my child is already living with a disrupted stress system? If I can't find affordable day care for my baby, is there a greater chance my baby will experience stress in a less desirable setting? How can I get my teenager the help she needs when she is so withdrawn? How do I support my student who is struggling with anxiety, anger, or behavioral problems if the school doesn't have a framework in place to address mental health issues? How can we decrease the stress in our family when we cannot afford to step off the treadmill even for a vacation? Is it too late to do something about the stress I've already experienced, potentially putting me at risk for a heart attack? What are the broader consequences of this epidemic? Is stress changing our basic nature, making it ever more difficult to mend?

In the coming chapters, I will go through the individual stages—from baby to toddler to adolescent to adult life—explaining the current science on stress and SDR for each age, as well as the best ways to integrate and respond to it in a variety of circumstances. With each chapter, the perspective will broaden until finally, in the last chapters, we will view our struggle with stress from a societal standpoint, giving us a firm sense of how we can change social policy to break this dangerous cycle that threatens us all.

2

DESTINED TO THRIVE, DESTINED TO STRUGGLE:

The Critical Period of Baby's First Year

BELIEVE IT OR NOT, WE used to think that the first year of life wasn't that important for a baby's social and cognitive development—that the big moments of social development came later, when the child was three or four years old. Well, it turns out, this was dead wrong: a number of fundamental changes can occur during that first-year window but not after. For example, some infants are literally "born anxious," either because excess stress experienced by the expectant mother causes stress methylation in the fetus—that is, the stress gene is locked in the "on" position—or because they inherited the stress-methylated version of the gene. But how their stress system functions can be altered by what they experience during their first year of life. Supernurturing—intense, patient, and empathic support—can actually overcome already existing SDR, even if it was inherited, and act as a buffer against the effects of early adversity. But the reverse is also true: high stress or adversity can lead to stress methylation in babies not born with it. Parents or primary caregivers play the central role here, but the broader social context—whether harsh or supportive—can also make a major difference. Let's turn now to how this plays out through the baby's first year.

In telling this story of stress to many different audiences, I have fielded all kinds of questions, but the most pressing ones have come from those who were either expecting a baby or were in the early stages of parenting. These mothers and fathers come to me at the end of almost every talk I give. While they're usually elated about starting a family, they are also almost invariably worried about the implications of what I've told them.

The expectant parents, who have sworn off alcohol during the pregnancy, banished nonorganic food from their fridge, and taken every manner of vitamin recommended by their obstetrician, can't believe they've got another thing to worry about, and to make matters worse, worrying itself and the stress it causes are part of the problem! They have a lot of stress in their lives—demanding bosses, long commutes, financial difficulties, not to mention the flood of advice about pregnancy. Could they be dooming their kids to a life of stress?

Then there are the parents who are already raising a baby, and struggling. Their concern is invariably telegraphed by tense facial expressions and weary eyes. Why can't their children seem to settle down? Why are they experiencing crying jags that go on for so long that it begins to feel like glass shattering over and over again? And what about things that have already happened— could the financial strain they felt after the husband was laid off have impaired their baby's stress system?

Across the board, these women and men want to know if their

children are going to experience the challenges of an amped-up stress system. And to all of them, I explain that stress does not discriminate. From the baby's perspective, it really doesn't matter *why* parents are anxious or stressed-out. What does matter is whether the stress reaches a high enough level during pregnancy or the early part of the child's life to trigger methylation.

Though we don't know precisely at what point this disruption of the stress system occurs, we do know quite a bit about what a baby needs in utero and during the first year of life to increase the odds of a healthy, successful future. So until we can identify more precise triggering levels, it makes sense to do everything we can within reason to meet the baby's needs in terms of nurturing and creating a low-stress environment. In this chapter, we will take a close look at what those needs are and the challenges parents face in meeting them in specific situations. What protective measures can be taken during pregnancy to prevent your baby from experiencing stress methylation in utero? What might cause stress-methylated SDR during the first year of life? What are the signs of SDR? And if the baby's stress system *is* turned on, what can be done to help shift the baby back in a healthier direction and protect or buffer the child throughout life?

EPIGENETIC MODIFICATION: HOW THE ENVIRONMENT ALTERS THE GENES

Before we get into the specifics of how to prevent or handle a disrupted stress system, it is important to understand that stress methylation doesn't actually alter the gene itself—the DNA stays the same. It does alter the way the gene is *expressed*—how it functions. The change is not genetic, but *epi*genetic: it acts on, but stands outside of, the gene. The stress gene, like many others, is designed to be turned on and off in response to the environment. Epigenetic modification affects the gene's on-off switch; it affects the way the gene is expressed. High levels of cortisol experienced by the fetus or the very young child can result in this specific epigenetic modification—stress methylation.

The epigenetic modification process, however, does not occur only with stress; it can occur with other genes as well, creating a variety of health complications. We now know, for example, that environmental toxins like tobacco affect the regulator on a gene that controls the growth of cells. When this switch gets shut off, there is a hyperproliferation of cells that can lead to cancer.

And yet there is a good reason why our bodies undergo epigenetic modification: it also plays a role in our survival. More than thirty years ago, scientists discovered that approximately 95 percent of our genes are not useful to us; over the course of evolution, they have become irrelevant. These genes are often referred to as "dark DNA" or "junk DNA." Within the first two weeks after conception, the fetus does a kind of sweep of its own body and, largely through the epigenetic process, shuts down the dark DNA; without this, the fetus wouldn't survive.

Although we've known about dark DNA for decades, the study of epigenetics (beyond the field of embryology) is relatively new. And the study of "social epigenetics"—that is, how the social environment can alter the way that the genes work—is an even more recently developed field. In fact, when Michael Meaney presented his group's findings about the rat pups deprived of maternal nurturing—thus allowing us to uncover the mechanism we'd been fervently hoping to find—he essentially launched social epigenetics as a new field of research. Soon after, many others began to delve into the ways in which social influences in early life can reshape our basic biology—and with lifelong consequences.

We'll focus in this book on the specific story of SDR, because it is a central link in the causal chain from early life adversity to SDR to inequality of outcomes in development, health, and longevity. And because we have the most complete scientific story for this type of epigenetic methylation. Over the last decade, more findings have linked early life adversity to additional social epigenetic changes that are also likely to prove problematic, such as a gene related to maternal nurturing behavior and another linked to the production of the "trust hormone," oxytocin. We will surely have a more complete picture of these social epigenetic effects in the near future, as research is growing very rapidly. Stress also operates directly on brain structure and function, as some very recent research has shown, including brain regions involved in learning (hippocampus), emotion (amygdala), and executive function (prefrontal cortex). Identifying the precise sources of all the effects that come from excess stress remains an intense focus for research.

So far, though, we haven't seen any *positive* impacts from early life adversity, other than preparing the individual for life in a highly dangerous environment. We want to avoid what evolutionary researchers call just-so stories—explanations custom-tailored to fit specific findings—but we can judiciously speculate that the social epigenetic effects of early life stress do seem to point toward a specific survival strategy for living in a dangerous world: stay on high alert all the time (stress), don't invest too much in any one offspring (maternal nurturance), and don't get too invested in others (oxytocin). You can see why this "epigenetic" advice could help you to survive long enough to reproduce, but at a pretty high cost to your own health and well-being.

In further examining the epigenetic process with regard to stress, we have come to understand that this altered gene can be passed down from generation to generation. If a new mother's mother experienced high levels of stress during *her* pregnancy, the new mother's stress response system may have become dysregulated when she was in utero. Or perhaps the new mother's parents were unable to provide the steady warmth and responsiveness that she needed as an infant, which can lead to biologically embedded stress dysregulation before she was born. This can even happen as a carryover from earlier generations. That is, if a mother has the methylated version of the stress gene, she can pass that along to her fetus independently of whether she is experiencing undue stress while pregnant. Consider it an epigenetic inheritance as opposed to a genetic inheritance. All of these different pathways lead to the same outcome: an amped-up stress response system.

A DEFINING TIME

Not so long ago, the prevailing idea was that very early development—in utero or the first year or so of an infant's life—wasn't all that important in terms of psychological consequences, except in the most dramatic cases of physical harm. But this assumption was based not on science but on adult perspectives. No one really remembers much, at least consciously, about what happened in the first year, so how important could it be? After all, a year or two is a tiny portion of a lifetime, a very small percentage on average, so why worry so much about early life stress and adversity?

Over the last few decades, however, an avalanche of evidence from the study of infant and early childhood development, based on research that followed large numbers of people from birth to adulthood, has shifted our understanding of this time completely. We now know that *there is no single period as important for life outcomes of developmental health as the period from conception to a child's first birthday.* We also know that a crucially important reason for this unique impact is biological embedding—changing an individual's biology during early life, affecting the broad range of developmental health, and having it persist across the lifespan. More specifically, it is during this time that the stress gene can be altered. Instead of dismissively saying, "They're just babies. They'll get over it," we now understand that this is a decisive stretch of time with many lasting results.

One of the most striking examples of this comes from the Romanian orphans study described in Chapter 1. When the scope of this tragedy came to light after Ceauşescu's regime ended, many of these children were subsequently adopted into families in other countries who could provide much improved circumstances. Later, some of these children participated in follow-up studies of their development.

The findings were straightforward: most of these children

were found to have higher levels of stress methylation and exhibited the behavior associated with it, such as acting out or withdrawing (most were inclined toward one or the other, but some alternated between the two) in early childhood. Stress methylation is not the *only* way to instigate these behaviors—genetic vulnerabilities can lead to a similar pattern, even if the exposure to stress is not nearly as severe. But those who were adopted within the first year of life showed much less disturbance, and in fact, by early to middle childhood, they were virtually indistinguishable from the average child—behaviorally, physiologically, cognitively.

Another study, published in 2016, looked at mothers and newborns in the war-torn Democratic Republic of Congo. Based on the women's own report of their experiences, researchers compared those who had suffered "war trauma"—primarily defined by being kidnapped or raped by soldiers—with those who had not. Though all the women described elevated stress, the babies belonging to the women in the trauma group showed significantly higher levels of stress methylation.

In yet another study, called Project Ice Storm, researchers found that stress affected not only babies born in war or other extreme circumstances, but also those born under much less severe conditions. Scientists from Quebec observed children of mothers who were pregnant during a major winter storm that stranded large numbers of families without power or transportation—and, in some cases, food—for several weeks in 1998. They found stress methylation effects in these children too, testing them several years after birth. Certainly, living without electricity or a way to get around town—and especially having to ask your neighbors to share their food, as many families had to do during this ice storm—are stress-inducing circumstances. On the other hand, this was a temporary situation and these were middle-class families with otherwise comfortable lives. So not only do we know that the period from conception through the first year of life is a significant and susceptible one for the stress response system, but we also know that stress methylation can occur under much less tragic circumstances.

LYNN, JEREMY, AND BABY JACK

When Lynn and Jeremy's firstborn son, Jack, was just turning three years old, his day care providers noticed that he was struggling more than other kids. He was more unwilling than the other kids to separate from Mom or Dad at the start of the day. He would often sit apart from the group on his own; he was often clingy with the teachers; and he was quite irritable off and on during the day, especially during transitions from one activity to another. When the day care staff, whom Lynn and Jeremy knew were experienced and caring, encouraged them to seek a professional consultation, they came to see a clinical colleague of mine.

My colleague interviewed Lynn and Jeremy to get a detailed developmental history. They were both in their early thirties, living in Seattle, and working in information technology. They had met in college and were married soon afterward. Jeremy had snapped up a promising position at a tech start-up group working on new apps; it offered a good income and solid prospects for making it big, but its long-term success was uncertain. Lynn agreed to take a more stable, middle-level job in a large, established firm, with an eye toward soon starting a family. Both were delighted when they learned they were going to have a baby.

But the stress on Lynn started to build soon after, on two fronts. Her mother, who lived in a small town in Ohio, discovered that she had advanced-stage cancer and probably only had a few months to live. Lynn began traveling to be with her mother, using much of the leave time she had been saving to extend her time at home after the baby arrived. And unexpectedly, Jeremy's start-up fell apart. Although they had managed to put away some savings, the speed with which it occurred left them reeling financially. To make matters worse, these events coincided with the collapse of the housing market and the financial downturn, which eliminated the option of using their home equity as a buffer. In short, Lynn recalled all of this as if it were a bad dream, except it was real, and remembered being a "total stress case" throughout her pregnancy.

When Jack arrived, they were of course delighted, but still dealing with significant stress and grief. Lynn's mother died when Jack was just a month old. They all traveled back to Ohio for the funeral and for Lynn, an only child, to help her father adjust to his loss.

Lynn and Jeremy later recalled that from the very beginning, Jack was very hard to soothe. Further, he had no regular sleep cycles even after a number of months, and he cried constantly, often exhibiting the piercing distress cry that by itself can bring the strongest parent to the edge of despair. To make matters worse, he had significant difficulty in breast-feeding, making a possible source of comfort yet another stressor.

For financial reasons, Lynn had to return to work when Jack was about three months old, much earlier than planned. With money tight and no other family nearby, Jeremy became the primary caretaker; he was also spending substantial time on maintaining professional networks and seeking a new position. Although Jeremy loved his son deeply and was invested in caring for him, stress from his perceived loss of status and actual loss of income began to take its toll. By Jeremy's own account, these circumstances led to a distant and somewhat perfunctory connection with Jack. Lynn's exhaustion, worry, and guilt about leaving Jack made her less available for the strong bond with him that she craved, and the strain also began to interfere with Jeremy and Lynn's connection and intimacy, allowing fewer avenues for dealing with the mounting stress. Their family embodied the vicious cycle that stress can launch.

Initially, Lynn and Jeremy put Jack's problems down to the disruption in their own lives, but as Jack grew, and their problems began to resolve, his behavior continued to be difficult for them and for him. They noticed that he was highly sensitive to even mild stimuli: a television turned on at too loud a setting could set him off on a crying jag or propel him to seek out and cling to Mom or Dad. He approached playgroups with a fear that they saw as significantly more pronounced than that exhibited by other friends' kids.

By the time Lynn and Jeremy brought Jack in to my colleague for a full evaluation, they were pretty worried. A thorough examination showed no clear signs of neurological or other limitations and identified the issue as one of a difficult temperament along with separation anxiety owing to the prenatal and early history that Jack had experienced. This is a classic description of the combination of an infant suffering with SDR and high-stress, disrupted parenting.

HOW MUCH STRESS IS TOO MUCH?

The pediatrician and psychoanalyst D. W. Winnicott developed the concept of the "good-enough" parent. But how far from good enough does parenting need to be to trigger this process? When worried parents approach me with this question after my talks, I respond with my own set of questions: How stressed do you feel on a daily basis? Do you often feel upset, agitated, or out of control? Do you feel your heart is racing much of the time? Do you feel physcially weighed down by worries? Do you feel like you can't think clearly, like you're walking through molasses? In many cases, your physiological response will give you a clue to as to whether you are flooding your system with cortisol.

But there were also those parents who described scenarios that were clearly not posing risk, such as the pregnant woman who'd recently become infuriated at her boss and had to swallow her anger or the mother who confessed to leaving her ten-month-old to cry in his crib one time because she couldn't soothe him. These women also wondered if they had affected their children's stress systems negatively. Typically, I would explain, one-offs or occasional events of that sort don't cause damage; it is the recurring stressor that is likely to disrupt the system.

But the bottom line is, we can't yet say exactly where to draw the line. For one, not every newborn is equally vulnerable, genetically. This shows up in the differences between "orchid" and "dandelion" children. Dandelion children are able to take root and survive under almost any circumstance, whereas the orchids—who have a distinctive genetic profile—are more fragile but, in the right environment, can bloom magnificently. Thus, the orchids will be more vulnerable to variations in parenting and can be harmed more easily by diminished or absent nurturing. On the other hand, these children are also more likely to excel when offered "supernurturing"—a term we came up with at CIFAR to mean consistently, even stubbornly, coddling a baby despite its protestations or unresponsiveness. The dandelions, however, might be able to get along fine with less attention. And yet these children with a more rugged constitution can also acquire SDR if they are pushed far enough. Virtually none of the Romanian orphanage children over the age of one year escaped that fate, even those fortunate enough to move to a much more comforting environment.

Another reason it is difficult to specify the moment that stress methylation might occur is that nurturing is such a broad term—it's hard to quantify or pin down. It's difficult to know whether one problem in parenting may be compensated for by another quality that is working well. That is, there can be cold but protective parenting, warm but less careful parenting, and so on. Research continues to focus on these and other variants of parental nurturing, but we don't have enough information yet to offer a perfect sense of what falls below the line of "good-enough" parenting.

That said, we *can* specify what children need early on, the protective factors that help our kids develop a functioning stress response system—as well as a sense of balance and, eventually, self-reliance. We also know that there are certain behaviors that can steady an infant or child with a compromised stress system and, in some stunning cases, reverse the effect of stress methylation altogether during the first year of life. Some emerging evidence from animal research also raises the possibility of reversing the methylation effect later in life through direct biochemical infusion that can break the bond. This potentially promising avenue of research is moving forward, but its relevance for humans is not yet clear. For children and adults, the evidence is that this biologically embedded change—stress methylation—to how the stress system works is highly stable.

Humans are social animals and we are dramatically affected by our relationships. I always mention to pregnant women who feel that they are at risk for stress themselves or parents who think they might not be able to tend to the needs of an infant, that social support in as many forms as possible—a grandparent, a babysitter, a neighbor, a close friend, a small group care situation—is one of the most important ways to decrease feelings of anxiety. Although we know this intuitively, we often underestimate the powerful ramifications these interactions have on our essential well-being. Extreme social isolation often leads to serious mental health issues, even for otherwise healthy people. It's why many religions use excommunication as the ultimate penalty—being forcibly removed from one's community is a powerful instrument of social control.

So it should be no surprise, then, that how we experience the social world in our earliest days would have such a dramatic impact. There are three experiences in particular that stand out as having striking results in terms of maintaining optimal mental health for a child: parental warmth and responsiveness; the attachment relationship; and the ability to self-soothe later on in life. For each of these, we will look at how the stress-methylated SDR pathway affects and is affected by the way the parent/child relationship plays out.

Is My Baby Stress-Dysregulated?

What are key signs of SDR to look for? Compared to other infants of the same age:

- Is my baby sensitive to and/or more easily startled by novel or sudden sights, sounds, or touch?

- Is my baby difficult to soothe or calm, even after needs have been taken care of (hungry, diaper change, wanting to be held)?

- Does my baby have trouble falling asleep or staying asleep?

- Does my baby have high levels of general irritability or negative affect?

When is it something else, and how do I check it out?
These characteristics are common among stress-dysregulated infants, but they may also indicate other problems not arising directly from SDR. Here are some signs it may be worth looking into more closely:

- No or minimal sustained eye contact during social interactions, no or few vocal expressions of joy or displeasure, and avoidance of social interaction can be early indicators of autism spectrum disorder (ASD). Autism Speaks has a checklist of things to look for at different ages: www.autismspeaks.org /what-autism/learn-signs/developmental-milestones -age.

- Excessive shyness around anyone who is not a primary caretaker and inability to be coaxed into interactions with others may be signs of SDR, but if these behaviors are persistent and unresponsive to repeated attempts to engage your baby, an underlying anxiety disorder may be the primary source.

- If you are concerned that the pattern you are seeing is more extreme or unusual, it may be advisable to seek help from a medical or child development clinic. Specific interventions are available for particular diagnoses, like ASD and anxiety, and often the sooner they begin, the better the result.

- Keep in mind, though, that there is a lot of variability among infants who do not have an underlying problem. In *Quiet: The Power of Introverts in a World That Can't Stop Talking,* Susan Cain has called our attention to a perfectly healthy pattern of introversion—being shyer and less likely to seek social stimulation than our exuberant and extroverted modern Western cultures seem to prefer. These infants may become agitated or fussy around overly intrusive caretakers or other adults who are seeking outgoing interactions when the baby isn't ready to engage. If a baby soothes more easily when direct attention moves away from them, there may be little to be concerned about.

- A good rule of thumb: if you're worried, follow your instincts. Parental concerns about development are often some of the most reliable indicators that something may be awry, and require further investigation. Be wary of individuals who attempt to minimize your concerns—well-meaning platitudes can cause self-doubt and increase parents' sense of isolation. Seek advice from professionals who understand how babies work. Knowing that there isn't a problem reduces stress in itself. Learning that there is a problem can increase stress initially but can lead to getting help that will move things in a more positive direction.

WARMTH AND RESPONSIVENESS

Extensive research shows that the most important elements of comfort in the first year of life are emotional warmth and responsiveness to an infant's needs. If you've had children or taken care of infants, you've likely had firsthand experience with the reality that babies enter the world with almost no capacity for self-soothing. They acquire the ability to control their emotions gradually during childhood and into adolescence, but in the beginning, their only recourse is to let the people around them know that something is not right. Which is to say, they cry. Pretty quickly, parents learn how to run through a routine that works to get their child back to a calmer, quieter state. Hungry? Need a diaper change? Need a cuddle and a bit of rock-a-bye? Need sleep?

Much of the time, this run-through works and all becomes well again—for a little while, anyway. Which is not to say it is without stress. Infants tend to run on their own schedules, not on their parents' timing, and the continuous monitoring, the feeling of constantly being on call, and, perhaps most crucially, the sleeplessness, come together to make this a high-anxiety experience. But what aspects of this matter most to the baby?

When a baby signals that something is amiss, it matters if the need is met fairly promptly, at least most of the time. This doesn't mean being at the infant's beck and call at every moment of the day or night, but it does mean that distress should lead to soothing in a reasonably predictable way for the baby. Why is it significant that a baby's needs be met when he lets you know he's unhappy? After all, if feeding, changing, and soothing are happening—regardless of whether this is happening at just the moment the baby is demanding it—shouldn't that be nurturing enough?

No, actually. Think of it this way: Something doesn't feel quite right to the baby, and so the stress system kicks in to signal that something is wrong. "I'm hungry," "I'm wet," "I'm lonely," or some other discomfort. Getting that need met in a timely fashion tells the baby that the world—or, at least, the baby's world—is predictable, reliable, and worth feeling good about. As that sense of faithfully being cared for—let's call it *trust*—starts to become internalized, the tolerance for delay increases gradually: "Mom or Dad will be here soon." This is not yet a self-aware process, of course, but it does establish the early neural links from stress to solution—and, over time, to self-soothing. More specifically, it turns off the stress signal, helping to establish the feedback loop that will be needed for later self-regulation—and to keep the stress response system in check.

Let's consider what happens when these signs of predictable nurturance are not present. Simulating circumstances in which a baby's needs are not met in scientific experiments are limited for ethical reasons, thankfully, but one technique that is often used in research focuses on the absence of social warmth with "the still-face paradigm." With this, the parent looks at a baby for a short period of time with no emotional expression at all. (When this is too difficult or upsetting for the parent, an experimenter presents a blank expression.) At first, most babies are a bit puzzled, but soon they begin to present their best, most adorable bids for emotional connection—smiling, laughing, gazing expectantly— all to no avail. Pretty soon, they become quite flummoxed, often launching into a full-bore cry. And what else happens? Their HPA axis kicks in, sharply raising their cortisol levels. Experiencing this pattern repeatedly can then lead to the methylation of the stress gene. It is the *repetition* of affectionate responsiveness—or its absence—that matters, rather than one-off events. If, at times, a mother or father or other caretaker simply can't respond right away, it's unlikely this will lead to methylation and its later problems. It is the constancy of this kind of behavior that is meaningful, the steady drip of everyday life.

And yet there are a number of understandable reasons for an absence of emotional warmth and responsiveness from parents. If the parent is suffering from serious depression—whether postpartum or chronic—the baby will sense that his caretaker is unavailable, and the stress system will be alerted. Well-intentioned interventions, like sleep training ("cry it out") have been shown to have, for young infants, the unintended consequence of increased cortisol release, with potential long-term effects. (One of the leading proponents, Richard Ferber, has subsequently clarified that this is not a recommended method for young infants.) If Mom and Dad can only be present intermittently, with alternate caregivers who are not emotionally available, the baby will sense that something is amiss. This is why, under these kinds of circumstances, it is extremely valuable to seek out a person or a small group of people who can consistently provide a reliably warm and responsive setting and look after the infant if the parents or primary caregivers are emotionally or physically unavailable.

Affection and attentiveness are so crucial because they help to create the basis for the development of brain chemicals that are a major buffer against stress. The first of these is oxytocin, known less formally as the "love hormone" or the "trust hormone." Few of us can resist a sentimental response when we see a picture of a mother with her baby in the crook of her arm, the two of them gazing into each other's eyes. But what *they* are experiencing at that moment is even more extraordinary. There is a surge of oxytocin for both parent and child that will reach one of the all-time peak levels in a lifetime. An even higher level occurs for both mother and child during breast-feeding. The ability to invoke these potent emotions—and attendant physiology—during moments of bonding creates a strong protection against SDR. It not only soothes and provides contentment but, amazingly, the oxytocin itself can mop up any cortisol that may be in the baby's system. In essence, oxytocin can absorb—and dispel—excess amounts of the stress hormone that may still be coursing through the body.

Serotonin, another neurochemical that is central to positive social connections, can mitigate both anxiety and consequent acting-out behaviors. A well-functioning serotonergic system, as with oxytocin, counteracts SDR, limiting the triggers of cortisol activation from mild stressors. A child who is neglected by a parent in infancy—or who doesn't feel attended to by a caregiver—is set on a course toward anxiety, depression, and mood disorders. Serotonin is a powerful antidote for these disorders, which is why medical treatment targets the serotonergic system. The widely used selective serotonin reuptake inhibitors (SSRIs) such as Prozac (fluoxetine), Paxil (paroxetine), and others, for example, are designed to make more of an individual's serotonin available to the key receptors in the brain, elevating

mood and preventing a slide toward depression. But when offered enough affection and attention in the first year of life, a
child's natural production of serotonin is heightened—this,
along with the release of oxytocin, makes for a strong defense
against stress from the very start.

ATTACHMENT

The parent—or caregiver or some combination of these adult
figures—plays the absolute role in offering warmth and responsiveness to a baby, but the attachment relationship is a two-
way street; both parent and child are active participants in
forming it.

If the baby has developed SDR in utero, this can cause a considerable strain on the parent-child bond from the get-go. If
you have cared for a baby like this, you know just how hard
things can get. These infants' needs will be greater because they
are much more sensitive to any discomfort: they are just a little
bit more out of sorts, more tired, more startled. As a result, the
parent-on-call button gets pushed more often. To make things
even harder, because these babies are born with their stress system already biologically embedded in the ON position, they are
more difficult to soothe. It's natural that a parent with a child
like this may get more than a little frustrated and pull away. No
matter how hard they try, they end up feeling like ineffectual
parents, because their baby doesn't respond to their efforts at
soothing. It's hard to develop a sense of mastery when efforts
to calm an infant don't work.

For these parents, walking, rocking, feeding, swaddling, and holding close—nothing is guaranteed to settle the baby. And, even after settling or falling asleep, it doesn't take much to get the baby going again. As I described earlier, warmth and closeness—and the oxytocin-serotonin cascade this can set off—offer a special kind of joy for both parent and baby. This is a natural evolutionary response; it is an essential reason why caring for a demanding newborn seems worth it. But what if that feeling is rare because the baby is so difficult to comfort, in large part because he's just not comfortable in his own skin? Then it becomes more challenging to maintain the commitment to monitoring and responding in a timely way.

Parents of these children are dealing with hard-to-soothe kids, their own fragile emotional state, and feelings of failure that result from this. So it's just the icing on the cake when they don't get the support *they* need. Efforts to express their feelings of frustration and sadness are sometimes met with judgment: "Well, you signed up for this, so if it's not as peachy as you thought it would be, tough—it's still your job." One of the things I hope will come out of understanding *why* these children are so hard to soothe is that parents will blame themselves less, seeking and, they hope, receiving support rather than judgment. They will also be freed from the inclination to make harsh attributions about why their baby is acting this way.

Despite all of these challenges, despite feelings of irritation or incompetence, many parents simply refuse to take no for an answer from their babies, swaddling and bouncing and holding them close—defiantly whispering "shhh, shhh, shhh"—in a relentless effort to calm them down. This is the essence of supernurturing. And this is exactly the right instinct, even as it's sometimes *very* hard. If this extreme comfort is provided early and consistently enough, it is just what these infants need to overcome their SDR inheritance.

But let's always remember that this is not easy to do, especially when there may be few supports available to new parents dealing with these circumstances. In this situation, others need to be called on to help out. As anthropologist Sarah Blaffer Hrdy points out in her book *Mothers and Others*, alloparenting— Hrdy's term for tending to infants and children by adults other than the biological parents—offers advantages to both mother and child. And effective nurturing by others also offers the same defense against SDR that is achieved from an attachment relationship with a parent.

In fact, along the lines of the Romanian study, there is evidence that an attentive nonbiological caregiver can fully reverse the effects of a maladapted stress system. Steve Suomi, the NIH researcher in our CIFAR network who brought us his crucial findings about the behavior of monkeys who had been deprived of maternal care, also discovered that monkeys born with a high probability of being anxious and reactive as well as possessing a hyped-up stress response system were given a second chance if raised by highly nurturing "foster" monkey mothers. These mothers allowed much more physical contact than usual, for months longer than would be typical. They were also less likely to react negatively if the infant acted aggressively. They did not, for example, swat them for pulling at the teat while feeding. In general, these mothers made room for a greater range of difficult behaviors from the babies they were caring for.

By the time these fostered monkeys were juveniles and adults, they showed standard behavior (in peer interactions especially) and physiology, with stress regulation functions and serotonin secretion rates similar to average monkeys. The only distinction appeared to be that they were more likely to attain high status in the troop by being good team players, highly aware of what was going on socially but not inappropriately reactive to it. As Steve explained, our intuitive notion that social status in primate groups—or human groups, for that matter—comes largely from dominance behaviors is actually quite wrong. More often than not, it comes from the more sophisticated path of building alliances and coalitions. Being on high alert and with a hair-trigger response, like SDR monkeys, runs against this; but keeping the ability to pick up on all the social interplay, without reacting aggressively or hiding away in fear, helps to facilitate the collaborative path to high status.

Supernurturing a Distressed Infant

What is supernurturing and how do we know it can help?

- Infants with SDR can be especially hard to parent effectively, because they present more than the usual challenges in soothability, irritability, and sleep disturbance and because they are able to provide fewer positives to caretakers that make the efforts to nurture seem more worthwhile.

- From animal studies, like those by Steve Suomi at NIH, we know that monkey newborns who present with this pattern can be turned around by foster moms who exhibit extraordinary patience day-to-day, and to extend the length of time they are willing to devote to careful, attentive, and involved nurturing.

- The later success of Romanian orphans who were fortunate to be adopted earlier in life, usually in the first six to twelve months, is a testament to a similar pattern of parental patience and investment of their adoptive parents.

- Recognizing that the challenges to parenting an infant with SDR are not a reflection on you as a parent is an important first step. If the typical parenting behaviors, with warmth and sensitivity, don't work as well for your baby as you have observed they do for others, it can be helpful to realize that "failure" is not the right way to look at it.

- It does mean, though, that you may need to expect to put more into the effort, and get fewer immediate rewards, in the form of calming, cooing, and contentment from your baby. Persistence in warm and sensitive responding despite those challenges, though, offer a hopeful pathway for overcoming the SDR pattern over time.

- A key part of this warmth and sensitivity in the first year is communicated through physical touch. If this helps to keep your baby from becoming agitated, you may want to do this more often than other babies may seem to need. This does make it harder to deal with everything else that needs to get done, so keep in mind the advice on respite and relief from other caretakers.

- The respite rule is important for another reason: stress and negative emotions are contagious. If you are feeling frequently stressed-out and agitated by this demanding task, your baby will probably pick up on that, too. This isn't to say that occasional frustration won't happen—it will—but it is frequent and intense stress that needs to be avoided when interacting with your baby.

- A general rule related to this is to pay attention to what your baby likes and dislikes and take your cues from that. Babies, just like adults, differ in the kind, tempo, and frequency of social and physical stimulation. What is joyful to some can be intrusive to others. (One exception, again, is if your baby seems to decline all social contact, including eye contact, and gets quite fussy on most bids. Check the possible signs of ASD, listed above, or consult with your pediatrician or family doctor about your baby's overall development.)

Tips for avoiding that hopeless feeling

- Recognizing what may be going on, and making a commitment to extra efforts on behalf of your baby, does not mean that it's easy.

- It's important to realize that it is exhausting to keep up the warm and sensitive approach, long after other babies will have been soothed and calmed— and to have it happen again and again. Getting relief and respite is crucial, whether it is from a parenting partner or from trusted caretakers.

- Understand that lots of folks will be offering unsolic- ited advice, some of which might be useful, but which often comes across as implicit—or even direct—criticism. Finding what works for your baby is the most important thing, so find ways to deflect unwanted (or ill-intentioned) input, but also be open to suggestions that seem worth trying.

- Don't hesitate to seek professional advice, from doctors, child development specialists, and others. Many public health agencies can provide valuable information and support in this crucial task. You don't need to go it alone.

Parental attachment is crucial to all babies, but especially to those whose stress system is working overtime. They need more buffers against stress reactivity, and find it harder to make use of the few they may have. This difficulty in connecting with others is likely to appear as they grow up. We carry our early assumptions about how relationships work—or why they don't work—forward in life. We develop an internal working model of future relationships; if we were lucky enough to have had a secure attachment in early life, then we go forth presuming that relationships work most of the time. And this is often self-fulfilling—we know intuitively as well as from research following infants into adolescence and adulthood that individuals with a history of secure attachment are usually more flexible and open to establishing relationships of trust. We assume that our partners, friends, or colleagues will provide the sense of connection that we remember from our earliest experiences. Of course, sometimes we're wrong, and learning to discern which people will return our feelings is a core skill that we begin acquiring in adolescence—sometimes painfully so. It is also a continuing challenge throughout adulthood, but if the groundwork for secure attachments has been laid, these setbacks can be met with hope and resilience.

CULTIVATING THE ABILITY TO SELF-SOOTHE

Responsive parenting and a successful attachment bond are the building blocks needed to learn how to take on the role of calming oneself. This is perhaps the most important skill for someone struggling with an altered stress system to acquire. Learning how to keep one's own emotions in check reduces the frequency with which the HPA axis kicks into gear—and it also decreases the duration of the stress response once it starts to spin out of control. This is also one of the most difficult skills to achieve for a child (or adult) with SDR, precisely because the stress response invokes the automatic fight-or-flight instinct, which is essentially the opposite of self-soothing.

Self-regulation is much like other body systems that help to stabilize us. Think of the many mechanisms our body has for thermoregulation, keeping our temperature at just about 98.6 degrees Fahrenheit. If we're too hot, we sweat, and the water on our skin evaporates, cooling us off. If we're too cold, we shiver, suddenly creating a lot of muscle activity and burning fat, warming us up. But we don't need to consciously think about this kind of regulation; it's built into the system. We don't choose to sweat or shiver; it just happens when our internal temperature goes outside set parameters. And not everyone's set point is the same: some people may sweat when others shiver. Thermoregulation doesn't work by pushing us in only one direction—it aims to achieve a balance for the individual.

Self-regulation of our feelings, thoughts, and actions works like these other regulatory systems in that it has the capacity to move up or down, to achieve a good functional balance. Sometimes we want to down-regulate, when we find ourselves in the middle of a heated conflict, for example, and an awareness kicks in that the fight is not worth it. But sometimes we want to up-regulate, to get excited enough about something that we want to achieve: think of athletes psyching themselves up before a competition, a businessperson before a big presentation, or an actor about to go onstage. But where self-regulation differs from thermoregulation or other automatic bodily systems is that we *can* affect it by our own choices—for example, by seeking support in a moment of crisis or high anxiety.

The journey toward self-regulation begins with the first days of life outside the womb and is further shaped by hidden regulators, a term that we used in CIFAR to indicate that the benefits reaped from these actions take place, just as with biological embedding, "under the skin." The advantages that hidden regulators confer may be invisible—but they are potent. And they will serve a child well when it comes time to stand on her own two feet, emotionally speaking, because they will have created a physiology that is inclined toward stability. There are three hidden regulators and, you will notice, they intertwine with the need for responsiveness among caregivers.

The first of these hidden regulators—the simple act of being held closely and regularly touched by a parent or caregiver—provides an external regulator for the child. The child has not yet developed an internal regulatory system, so touching her is what settles her reliably at this point. Studies of cultures where infants are held closely nearly all the time, such as the !Kung San tribe in Africa, show that the crying and fretting rate is markedly lower than in typical Western societies. Babies are carried in a sling during the day, and nighttime cosleeping with parents is the norm in this culture. For even minor fretting, the baby is comforted within ten seconds on virtually all occasions. This is not the only way to achieve a positive outcome—it's not realistic to expect a parent in our culture never to put their baby down, and cosleeping on modern mattresses may carry its own health risks—but it hints at why consistent affection and responsiveness is a major part of stabilizing the stress response. It also emphasizes the substantial cost of nonresponsiveness to an infant.

Additionally, there is a great deal of research on newborns consigned to neonatal intensive care units that proves the power of human touch. Multiple studies have shown that regularly stroking and touching infants in incubators helps to regulate their physiology—and, in certain cases, it can even make the difference between life and death.

The second hidden regulator, the oxytocin system, or the love hormone, is, as described earlier, activated on close physical contact, with especially high rates during breast-feeding, and is a powerful counterforce to the excess cortisol from the stress response system. This early tuning up of the oxytocinergic system is likely to be of lasting benefit physiologically and emotionally; it will take a child a good distance in achieving self-regulation.

The third major hidden regulator is a bit more complicated: sucrose. The consumption of this sweet-tasting nutrition quickly counteracts cortisol in the body, whether through breast-feeding or by formula. In contrast to the other hidden regulators, however, which continue to be good for us in the long term, this sweet (and often fatty) approach to cortisol reduction comes with risk as well as calories. This is why we reach for comfort food when we're stressed—because we instinctively crave something sweet or fatty to counteract, or mop up, the cortisol pumping through our body. The evidence is rapidly growing that the link between high stress, both chronic and acute, and obesity is connected to the body's urge for sucrose, often through carbohydrates as adults, as a way to regulate cortisol. Relying on comfort food is in fact a kind of self-medication, because it reduces the immediate sensations of agitation and anxiety; but over the long term it's a path to diabetes, cardiovascular problems, and other related illnesses.

There is also a subset of this hidden regulator: nonnutritive sucking. This is, put more simply, when a baby is soothed by a pacifier or by her own thumb. Not as powerful in reducing stress as the other hidden regulators, it is still a useful tool. Research shows that for an agitated infant, vigorous sucking lowers the physiological stress response. But just as our early introduction to sucrose can lead us to crave comfort food as a way to combat stress in adulthood, pacifiers too can contribute to unhealthy adult oral fixations such as nail-biting.

Still, all of these early hidden regulators reliably reduce the stress response—and, ideally, help to move the developmental pathway toward other internalized forms of regulating emotions and behavior. A baby, for instance, who starts to suck his own thumb is exhibiting an act of self-soothing that is drawn from, and expands on, an early sense of stability and comfort. And, though this is more difficult to achieve with a child with SDR, it is possible with a bit more patience and time—essentially with supernurturing—to achieve the same effects.

We also need to understand that the ability to self-regulate, whose foundations rest on these early, hidden regulators, is the accumulation of many parent-child interactions over time, rather than one or a few singular occasions. This is what we have come to call the "steady drip of everyday life"—especially apt because the biology so often involves biochemicals that circulate throughout the system. Excessive worrying about one single interaction that didn't go well can be counterproductive if we let it get to the point where we ourselves are getting stressed because the stress itself becomes contagious.

NURTURING THE FAMILIES

It is crucial to note that families should not have to go it alone when it comes to finding the support that is necessary for the early bond between parent and child to develop smoothly. Later, I will take up the question of why society should make the investment in supporting stressed-out infants and families. There are utilitarian reasons; not accommodating this increases the overall social and economic burden on health and competence. There are also self-serving reasons, because as more families are struck by SDR, it becomes harder to maintain stability within the society at large. Whether we are motivated by reducing the overall health burden or reducing the risk to ourselves and our families, it is clear that the culture must play a role in backing families as they go through this influential period in developmental health.

Some Resources for New Parents of Distressed Infants

Daniel Siegel and Mary Hartzell, *Parenting from the Inside Out,* Tarcher/Penguin, 2003.

Myla and Jon Kabat-Zinn, *Everyday Blessings: The Inner Work of Mindful Parenting,* Hachette, 2014.

Pat Harvey and Jeanine Penzo, *Parenting a Child Who Has Intense Emotions: Dialectical Behavior Therapy Skills to Help Your Child Regulate Emotional Outbursts and Aggressive Behaviors,* New Harbinger, 2009.

Ruth Newton, *The Attachment Connection: Parenting a Secure and Confident Child Using the Science of Attachment Theory,* New Harbinger, 2008.

Harvey Karp, *The Happiest Baby on the Block (Revised 2nd Edition),* Bantam, 2015.

3

INTO THE ARENA:

The Social World of Peers and Schools

MOST KIDS HEAD OFF TO school at four or five years of age, whether to preschool or kindergarten. Even for those with previous experience with day care, this transition presents significant challenges: being away from home for a good part of the day, meeting the expectations of new adults, figuring out the social world of peers. It's for good reason that education researchers use the K-to-3 period as a benchmark to measure academic and social progress.

Not surprisingly, this period of major change provides a particular set of challenges for kids with SDR. Children with amped-up stress systems face a double bind: they have a harder time to begin with, and typical manifestations of their condition—quick to anger, feeling anxious and overwhelmed—make it harder to deal with the expectations of school successfully. Add to this the invidious comparisons to other kids, which bring more stress to them and their parents. You can see why they can seem destined to struggle.

Fortunately, parents and schools can do specific things to help—even though the core biology of SDR is unlikely to change, whether that arose from stress methylation or not. Helping SDR kids acquire coping skills that lessen or even overcome the effects of SDR is a central goal. Parents continue to exert the most important influence, and supporting them in that effort needs to be a key goal. Bringing others into the child's orbit beyond the immediate family, though, presents new opportunities to build resilience. It's critical for parents of SDR kids to make such opportunities for resilience more available and more likely to be taken up as a key goal for these kids.

If you are a parent you know that parenthood involves a never-ending series of BIG decisions accompanied by the dread that the wrong move may have lasting negative consequences. And high among these decisions are those involving early child care. When should it begin? Should I stop working to take care of my child until she's older? What setting will be best for my child? Can we find a good public school? And, as if that weren't enough, a stream of conflicting expert opinions run throughout the process: Children should stay at home with parents as long as possible. High-quality care is a benefit for many children. It is best to delay or repeat kindergarten for kids who are younger than most at the start of school. And so on.

These battling claims became confusing enough that, in 1991, the National Institutes of Health launched a major longitudinal study of early child care, looking at more than a thousand infants from birth through childhood and adolescence. Researchers observed their development in a number of crucial areas, such as their ability to form strong connections with people, cognitive development, educational achievement, and behavioral problems. This landmark study found two things of particular significance to parents. The first was that children who had experienced high amounts of out-of-home care from very early on—an average of more than thirty hours per week throughout the first four years of life—were somewhat more likely to show behavioral issues, especially difficulties with acting out in their first years of school. But this finding came with an important caveat: even if the child did spend the specified number of hours outside of the home, aggressive behavior increased only to a modest degree.

The study's second significant finding revealed that children in higher-quality care tended to perform only a bit better on academic and language skills at the start of elementary school than those in lower-quality care. This was especially true for kids on the bottom end of the socioeconomic scale. (The quality of the day care was measured primarily through direct observation by the researchers.) But, once again, the results were modest.

In the big picture, then, parents could take some relief: in fact, there are not dramatic impacts based on these early child care decisions.

The biggest discovery that emerged from this study was not about child care at all. Knowing that the style of parenting was likely to have an effect on their results, the researchers closely observed parent-child interactions of the families involved throughout. And, as it turned out, differences in parenting had a much larger impact on a child's development than the assorted arrangements in child care; in fact, parenting choices were found to be as much as ten times more important. Additionally, the mildly negative effects of large amounts of care outside the home were enhanced in families with less effective parenting. The parenting that made the difference was the kind discussed in Chapter 2: secure attachment, warm and responsive interactions with the child, and support for developing self-regulation skills.

What these findings underscore is that the familial relationship continues to be the primary factor in a child's development beyond the critical period of infancy. The main requirement of parenting with babies is to be warm and responsive; this helps the baby to develop a healthy attachment with the parent and the ability to develop social connections that will, in turn, support health and well-being later on. This relationship also acts at a biological level, deploying neurochemicals to absorb any excess cortisol produced by high-stress responses. And all this continues to be true through early childhood and beyond— except now children will also begin to take their first few steps, emotionally speaking, away from their parents.

MOVING TOWARD INDEPENDENCE

Starting from the time children are about two to three years old they gradually become more independent from their parents. Small shifts toward the child's autonomy—from learning to play on one's own to asking for comfort from a parent when needed—build on the advantages conferred by a warm relationship and the hidden regulators proffered in earliest infancy. The child gradually becomes more independent, moving toward full independence during adolescence. A good way to view your role as parent or caregiver throughout this time—which will continue to be fairly hands-on until late adolescence in the normal course of development—is as scaffolding, like the supporting structure that is used in constructing a building until it is strong enough to stand on its own.

There are clear steps parents can take to help a child move toward independence. These are helpful to all kids—as they are building blocks of healthy development—but they are especially important for those dealing with an overactive stress system. By the time the child hits roughly a year old, it's not likely that SDR can be fully reversed, but it is clear that nurturing relationships continue to ease negative effects. And there are valuable habits that a parent can both practice and teach their children that will minimize the occasions, duration, and impact of excess stress regardless of the reason for the SDR, whether from stress methylation, genetic vulnerability, or some other source.

MAKING CHOICES

In early childhood, learning how to make simple decisions is a good step toward independence. Rather than asking your young child, "What do you want to wear today?" it is better to simplify the process for the child. You could ask, for example: "Do you want your blue shirt or your green shirt?" while holding both up. Offering a choice not only gives kids a sense of agency—and prevents a whining protest, "But I waaaanted to wear my green shirt!"—it also provides the child an opportunity to exercise his or her judgment within reassuring constraints. For the SDR child, however, this can be a major challenge. Even mild constraints, such as limiting choice to the blue or green shirt, can be taken as enough of an obstacle to launch the stress response, perhaps in the form of a temper tantrum or a quiet refusal to cooperate. Once it starts, this cycle is hard to interrupt, amplifying the cortisol release that prompts further challenging behavior. Parents of these children will have to walk a fine line between sticking to their request and helping the child tamp down his stress response. And many parents of kids with this SDR pattern dread trying to navigate this outside the home, where there is ample opportunity for strangers to roll their eyes or even make explicit comments on one's parenting efforts without knowing anything about the reasons for the child's behavior.

For any parent, a time-out or a simple consequence—such as no television in the afternoon—if delivered in a calm and straightforward way, can offer the child an escape from the grip his emotions have on him. For parents of children with amped-up stress systems, however, these episodes might happen more frequently and take longer to resolve. In this situation, during a time-out, for example, the parent might sit with the child in his room, waiting patiently until he is able to quiet down on his own. Even if this takes letting the child thrash about for a while until he has exhausted himself, this relays an important message. By not engaging with the angry behavior, the parent shows that it's not effective, and research shows that this will minimize tantrums in the future. And draining as it may be, the parent also demonstrates that there is a way out of the trap of stress and the child is able to find his own way to it.

TALK TO ME

Talking to children also cultivates self-regulation. In infancy, a parent's voice is a source of solace and comfort—it's why singing babies to sleep while carrying or rocking them is so effective. But regularly conversing with very young children, even before they're capable of a verbal response, also offers lessons about decision making, controlling their behavior, and understanding emotions.

New technology—namely, placing a very small recording device on the wrist of a child (with the consent of the family, of course) for a twenty-four-hour period—has allowed researchers to observe family interactions much more intensively. (In the past, they generally relied on diaries kept by the parents, which offered less material as well as less objectivity.) In studying these recordings, researchers have found that parents on the higher end of the socioeconomic scale speak more frequently to their children, confirming what the diary studies had shown over a number of years. In fact, these kids typically hear ten times the amount of language at home—before they even go to elementary school—than those from families on the bottom of the socioeconomic ladder. In addition, the families that talk more to their children tend to give clear explanations for *why* they are asking their children to do things, something like: "It's not as comfortable to play on the wood floor, so I'm going to move you over to the carpet." And they offer more lessons in labeling emotions as well: "You seem disappointed right now. Let's see what we can do about that." There is not only comfort in these communications; they are also useful ways to help children understand reasoning and emotion. Even the opportunity to make basic choices—like which shirt to wear—is more common among these families. Of course, no parent is perfect. When the stress is on ("We have to get into the car *now!*"), most will resort from time to time to the classic "Because I said so!"

But the broader point is that all parents can and should aim to narrate daily routines to young children—as well as expectations, plans, choices, and so on—in an age-appropriate way, helping the child to learn preparation and organization as well as beginning to sense how they might do this for themselves. Interestingly, this verbalizing about choices ("Would you like a grilled cheese or a PBJ for lunch?"), plans ("After lunch, we're going to the store."), and so on sets the stage for a useful skill for self-regulation: internal dialogue. Children learning how to handle a more complex world will often talk to themselves, which is very helpful. As we get older, we learn to submerge this self-regulation skill so it becomes inner dialogue, although it will burst forth from time to time, as in: "Where in the world did I leave my keys? I'm sure I put them down when I came in, but . . . ?" Or: "Right, the instructions say, 'Put dowel A into slot F,' so where is slot F?"

STICK TO A ROUTINE

Variability can be unsettling for kids since it means they're never sure what's going to happen next. For SDR kids, routines can provide a sort of "safety net" about what to expect. Many of these kids, in fact, have particular trouble dealing with unexpected changes. A reliable schedule provides an example that helps them to move closer to independence. "I'm kinda hungry," a child might think, "but I can see Dad making lunch." If, when hunger sets in, he can see that food is on its way, he can use the limited amount of self-soothing skills he has to stay calm until he is fed. This not only allows him to exercise this capability, but it means he begins to regularly anticipate that his needs will be met—an essential step toward impulse control and the capacity to delay gratification.

Some kids even let their parents know when they have strayed too far from routine. By the time she was about eighteen months old, one of my children used to ask to be taken to bed if we let the evening activities meander too far past bedtime. The flip side of structure and routine, of course, is disorganization and chaos. There is abundant research to show that this style of family life poses serious risks for a wide range of developmental health outcomes, such as a disrupted attachment between mother and baby in the early years. Few people actively seek a chaotic home life; it is most often a sign of parents pulled in too many directions. But the more you can hew to a routine in some form—even if it is simply getting kids to school on time or into a reliable child care situation—the better it is for everyone. When a child's ability to manage for himself is still in its early stages, routines provide predictability, and that keeps him from feeling nervous about what will—or won't—happen next.

And yet in all the conversations I've had with folks over the years, I don't recall any parents with a young child who said that chaos and difficulty sticking to routines *didn't* happen occasionally in their family. This rings true for almost every parent for a reason. Sticking to a routine is always a challenge when young children are in the mix. But there are great advantages, especially for the SDR child, to consistently making an effort in that direction, even if only with mixed success. Any predictability provides an anchor that helps to ground the stress response. If you never know what's coming, anything can seem like a threat. In fact, other advantages sometimes inherently follow maintaining some rituals. There is ample evidence, for example, that simple bedtime routines that involve reading to the child provide the double benefit of making restorative sleep more likely (for the whole family) and increasing school-readiness skills. Meanwhile, sleep requires a drop in cortisol, so there is a direct improvement for kids struggling with stress as well.

Although keeping to a routine may seem straightforward, we all know it isn't that simple. There are lots of potential interruptions to best-laid plans, and sometimes going outside the routine leads to fun interactions. So sticking rigidly to a routine is not always possible or desirable. But having a routine and then explaining the reasons why we're going off the routine on this specific occasion (and what we're doing instead) still provides a reliable anchor for dealing with change. And remember: routines are for the family, not just the child. This joint effort contributes to "mindful parenting."

BOUNDARIES AND EXPECTATIONS

At this point, too, there is a new aspect to parenting that comes into play in a big way: the setting of boundaries and expectations for positive behavior. Most of us are aware of the need to set boundaries and expectations, and that they are a crucial part of helping your child transition though developmental stages. Indeed, hundreds of studies over decades have bolstered this view: the combination of warm, responsive parenting with age-appropriate expectations and boundaries, known in the field as "authoritative parenting," leads to better outcomes for the child and the adolescent in everything from academic achievement to self-esteem to deeper friendships.

When a child responds to a parent's request and is rewarded with encouraging words—"You did that all by yourself. Good for you!"—this fosters a positive sense about taking control and mastering basic tasks. Parents sometimes interpret boundaries and expectations as being a negative thing—stinting on happiness or hampering creativity—but they are actually comforting to most kids. They provide a safe sense of exploration, without the feeling of unpredictability and the "anything goes" worries that go along with few or no limits.

In the case of a child with an amped-up stress system, however, authoritative parenting can be misinterpreted in both directions. Stressed-out kids are not always receptive to warmth or praise, and parents can be hurt or even angry when their affectionate praise is not met with a positive reaction. Thus, for parents of SDR kids, it's important to understand what's going on. For the child, boundary setting may be perceived as overly controlling or threatening.

Imagine yourself a child with SDR in the midst of an incident that triggers a fight-or-flight response. Your parent comes up to you and says, "You need to turn off the TV now. You know the rule: you have to tidy your room first." At this moment, you may perceive that typical parental expectation as an aggressive, threatening action. The parent will usually see the resulting acting out or extreme sulkiness as out of bounds and impose a punishment or consequence. That's why it's crucial for parents of SDR kids to be hyperaware that their child is viewing them from an entirely different perspective.

When parents are aware, however, of such potential miscommunications, they can help to steer both themselves and their children toward a calmer state. In these cases, it's best to step back, let emotions cool, and then try a variety of the practices listed above. Offer a choice: "I am still not going to allow you to stay up late to watch the movie tonight, but we can talk about watching it together this weekend." Talk it through: "It's a school night so you need to get to sleep on time in order to feel good tomorrow." Maintain a routine: practice this regularly until boundary setting doesn't trigger a negative reaction. Lastly, if after the conflict has passed, the child is seeking comfort, use this as an opportunity to affectionately reconnect.

Parents who come up against these clashes often, or who find the process taxing, might want to take a break every once in a while, asking a spouse or grandparent or friend to help out. In this case, however, it is important that the alternate caregiver offers continuity by asking that the same set of expectations be met. If a mother steps out of a lengthy conflict, for instance, only to have her husband give in to the child's demands, her hard work will be undermined and the lesson goes unlearned.

There is a more general point worth emphasizing here, especially given the strong evidence that this period of child development is still largely influenced by parenting: it is important to avoid developing a sense that every mistake you make—every routine you fail to keep, every boundary you fail to fortify—is going to doom your child. Although kids are highly sensitive to their social environments, the experiences that alter stress systems are generally not one-time, massively influential events. Some highly traumatic events can alter fundamental physiology and psychology, but this is more along the lines of severe abuse. Far more frequently, changes are shaped by the steady drip of everyday life. Patterns almost always become embedded with repetition. Routines not only shape how we think and act, but also affect the amount of cortisol—or serotonin or oxytocin—that is produced. It is the balance between them that makes a lifelong difference. So parents can let themselves off the hook for the isolated screwup or flameout (so long as there is no actual abuse, of course). What we need to be more aware of are the consistent habits and actions that quietly sculpt our children's minds and lives—as well as their underlying biology.

STEPPING INTO THE WORLD

At the moment kids enter formal schooling—kindergarten for most in the United States—children begin to experience significant new social opportunities and hurdles, which tend to increase in difficulty as they get older. Obviously, for kids who have trouble managing stress, these hurdles feel significantly higher. Failure to clear them can result in a difficult feedback loop in which failure reinforces itself. Children whose behavior makes it difficult to fit into social groups, because they aggravate the other kids or because they withdraw owing to their own anxiety, lose out on the practice needed to get better at social interaction. Like any other kind of skill, social competence develops into proficiency only with the opportunities to practice.

Among the most difficult of these new hurdles is a welcome to the world of social status. First, there is the rapid emergence of social dominance at school. This phenomenon surfaces in the first few months of kindergarten—which may seem startlingly early but is well established by research. Some kids establish themselves as particularly able at answering the teacher's questions, others at making friends. Very quickly, virtually all kids in a group can tell you everyone's position in the social hierarchy of the class, and whether they are near the top, bottom, or somewhere in between. Most parents try to direct kids away from thinking in terms of dominance or submission, but studies show it's virtually impossible to avoid.

At the same time, kids start to become aware of where everyone's family is situated on the broader socioeconomic scale. Even in kindergarten, they know who lives in the biggest house, goes on the nicest vacations, or has the latest pair of sneakers. These are the early stages of learning how to navigate these status comparisons, as well as how to view oneself in the bigger picture of society. This is complicated, even for adults. High family SES doesn't always translate into high social status in the kid world, or vice versa, but they're not completely independent either.

One of the most important ways for kids (or adults, for that matter) to succeed in social groups is to form alliances with others rather than trying to dominate them. SDR kids tend to struggle in the status game because their social interactions are often highly unpredictable, even to themselves. Social hierarchies, whether among kindergartners or rhesus monkeys, rely far less on strength and aggression than on learning how to build alliances and coalitions. A hair-trigger stress response—whether as fight (grabbing or shoving) or flight (withdrawing into a corner and isolating oneself from the others)—is a definite drawback in this game. Most kids are trying to protect or build their own status, and allying with an SDR kid obviously doesn't work in this direction. The path from SDR to social exclusion and isolation is often all too smooth. From here, substantial evidence shows that this can too easily cascade into syndromes or disorders of the externalizing (angry and acting out) or internalizing (anxious or withdrawing) types.

This time of transition to formal schooling is often the time when parents first truly realize that their child with SDR doesn't handle stress like other kids. Before this, many kids will not have experienced the kinds of stressors—both social and academic—that are a normal part of being in school. This often leads to stress responses that are easier to notice, like high levels of peer conflict or refusing to go to school. And until this point, most parents will not have seen their child in circumstances that would allow comparisons with other kids' behaviors. A member of our group at CIFAR who studied physical aggression from early childhood through adulthood noted that preschool is when the frequency of hitting, kicking, biting, and the like—for all kids—is at its peak. But, typically, this behavior drops off noticeably around three or four years of age—except for many SDR kids, whose behavior is the manifestation of the always-on fight-or-flight response. Alternatively, the flight response is expressed by withdrawal—since this is less disruptive, it's not as widely spotted as a problem. But it, too, should be recognized as a sign of an overactive stress system.

Both of these patterns—which child psychologists have named externalizing and internalizing syndromes—have been linked to hyper-HPA activity producing excess cortisol. Looking back at my early experience with both Jason and David, I realize now that they were most likely dealing with amped-up stress systems. Everything would be going along smoothly, but then, in response to something not obvious to others, they would suddenly act out. It seemed like Jekyll and Hyde to the rest of us. Once the HPA axis activates—which can feel like fear or anger or panic to a child—it's very hard to turn off the feelings. So it will be that much harder to come back to a calm resting state. While the behavior of a child suffering with SDR can seem out of control, it's not just a question of failing to achieve "mind over matter"; rather, the overreaction springs from biology.

This problem is also often compounded by the fact that these kids sometimes discern hassles or conflicts where others see only neutral behavior, leading them to misjudge the intent of parental interventions. This stems from a psychological perception typically associated with SDR that is called the "hostile attribution bias." This phenomenon, which has been extensively researched among children, can have catastrophic effects on a child's ability to make friendships and form alliances. In one such study, a scripted video shows an incident in which a child does something that could be interpreted as either accidental or purposeful; he bumps into another kid on the playground or in the cafeteria line, for example. When asked what happened, the child with a hostile attribution bias is quick to assign blame: "Yes, he clearly meant to bump me; it was on purpose." Meanwhile, other children witness the same scene and regard it as an accident.

Feeling emotionally on edge in this way can also interfere with learning. The connection between excess cortisol and learning problems may be even stronger than we previously thought; recent research shows a connection between early adversity and changes in the hippocampus, the part of the brain responsible for acquiring, honing, and maintaining new skills. SDR also plays a role in attention disorders: if you are preoccupied with defending against threats, real or imagined, you are going to have fewer mental resources for other things—and, of course, with mental struggles such as anxiety and depression. Difficulties with one—or as is often the case, more than one— of these areas become self-reinforcing, because these traits are themselves cause for stress.

For instance, a six-year-old who cannot pay attention for long periods of time because of an amped-up stress system may begin to fidget and interrupt the class, continually annoying the teacher and her fellow classmates. Rather than finally calming down as the result of being reprimanded or chided by friends, she grows increasingly *more* stressed, and therefore even less able to focus. These cycles are often hard to break, because they have what are known in scientific lingo as "strong attractor states." In simple terms, this means that there are many things—the inevitable jockeying for position among friends, the inherent difficulty in learning new skills, an overreaction to challenges— that pull kids back toward a long-established negative pattern in their brain. So it is hard to find something with enough oomph to break the loop and achieve escape velocity in a more promising direction.

A CULTURE OF RESILIENCE

And yet school is one of the few social institutions that can potentially offer a powerful new opportunity for highly stressed kids to assuage their emotions. For children who haven't—or weren't able to—form a secure bond with a parent or caregiver at home, school offers another chance at finding a beneficial relationship. Often teachers can serve as this kind of positive surrogate, strongly connecting with a child who lacks the attention he needs in his immediate family. In general, teachers who play this role embody the same traits of highly nurturing parenting: warmth, sensitivity, responsiveness, as well as a commitment to setting clear expectations and offering the support for meeting them. This kind of alliance can offer a child a shot of resilience, providing the necessary motivation to detour from some of the more negative paths of the mind. In Emmy Werner's study of high-risk kids in Hawaii, it was often the connection to a teacher, coach, or mentor in school that offered a way out toward achieving success that had seemed so elusive.

JACK GOES TO SCHOOL

We met Jack, the young boy struggling with the disruptions in his parents' lives, in Chapter 2. A couple of years after last consulting with my colleague, his parents, Jeremy and Lynn, returned, as Jack was struggling with his transition to first grade. In some ways the news was good: he had improved since the last time they'd met, less clingy and more willing to enter into the social world. Not surprisingly, the family's overall level of stress was much lower, as Jeremy had landed a high-profile job, enabling Lynn to move to part-time employment with a flexible schedule. She was spending more time with Jack and believed that this had led to a much stronger emotional connection between them. Lynn and Jeremy both said that their relationship had regained its closeness as well, further reducing their overall stress. And Jack's kindergarten experience had been positive, in part as a result of his having had a good relationship with a very involved and caring teacher. Jack still acted out, occasionally losing control of his emotions, but the teacher saw his behavior as a challenge worth addressing, giving him affection and helping him integrate with a circle of friends. They, too, began to appreciate Jack's strengths and interests. And Jeremy and Lynn, less overwhelmed by life circumstances, began to see him as something more than a constant source of stress. They could focus on his growing skills in learning and in getting along with others, and less on his problem behaviors.

You can imagine Jeremy and Lynn breathing a sigh of relief as Jack successfully completed kindergarten. He was finally on a path that seemed to promise a happy childhood. But first grade brought new challenges that made clear that big transitions were still really hard for Jack, and more generally that they weren't yet out of the woods. The increased academic pressure that came with first grade unsettled Jack deeply. He also began to struggle more with the complex game of social status. Lynn and Jeremy sensed that his new teacher wasn't as nurturing, but was instead more attuned to a competitive social dynamic. Regardless of the reason, Jack began to regress to his old SDR ways.

He was again oversensitive to mild stimulation. He was often irritable, he slept poorly, and he again became clingy with his parents. All of these things in turn interfered more and more with his academic and social development. His peers began to avoid and exclude him because it was harder to predict or understand what was going on with him.

As my colleague explored the family's difficult situation, she discovered that they had some strengths—in Jack, in his family, and at school—that could be built on. Working with the family, my colleague helped them to explore how to take advantage of those opportunities.

And take advantage they did. The school had instituted an evidence-based program for all the students, focusing on socioemotional learning and self-regulation skills—precisely the skills that Jack would need to turn things around. My colleague encouraged Lynn to learn the techniques taught in the program so that she could reinforce and amplify them. The school encouraged parent involvement, so she volunteered to start a robotics club, one of Jack's passions and an area she had worked in. With a group of like-minded peers and with Lynn working with the group, Jack began to regain his confidence in learning as well as his social skills. The teachers noted the shift in Jack's behavior and engagement and were patient in minimizing the difficult behaviors he still showed from time to time, although with decreasing frequency. By the end of first grade, Jeremy and Lynn, and Jack's teachers, felt that his progress toward resilience had come a long way. Still, they recognized that it would always be a struggle for Jack, and that they would need to be alert to his needs as new and tougher challenges come along in the future.

. . .

Just like Jack's parents, Jeremy and Lynn, most parents of kids who show the SDR pattern worry about is whether any of their efforts will make a difference in the long run. Supporting your child in the moment, working hard to build a support system to help them develop in healthier ways, can keep you focused on what's working or not working right now. But the nagging worry is whether this will help in the long run: Will your child eventually acquire the self-regulation skills to succeed on his or her own terms?

Fortunately, the evidence is quite clear that there are real prospects for this kind of long-term success. The research that shows this focuses on what we think of as resilience. Resilience has become a key focus of researchers and a virtual obsession for many parents, so it's helpful to understand what it really means. The psychologist Ann Masten, who has devoted much of her career to studying the subject, offers some important distinctions to keep in mind in her 2014 book *Ordinary Magic*.

We can start with what motivated some of the initial research, specifically the observation that some kids who have clearly experienced high levels of early life adversity—with multiple risks from economic and social disadvantages—nevertheless succeeded impressively in their later lives. We know that in general these kids show a higher frequency of SDR—and in a few recent studies, a higher incidence of stress methylation—but despite this, they manage to bounce back (the original meaning of resilience).

The obvious and important next question, especially for worried parents, is, "Can we figure out what leads to resilience?"

Masten uses the term "ordinary magic" to characterize the relationships in everyday life that help propel troubled children forward. There is quite a bit of evidence to back this up, as we've seen. As Emmy Werner found in her long-term study on the Hawaiian island of Kauai, and as Masten and many others have confirmed, establishing a restorative personal relationship—with a teacher, a coach, a mentor such as a Big Brother or Sister, and later on, a good friend or romantic partner—can help to diminish the effects of an overactive stress system, in particular the difficulties of creating subsequent attachments in life. These are especially important when the connection between parent and child has been problematic, frequently because of stresses on the parents that have made them less available than they would have preferred. Parents can redirect their efforts, as Jeremy and Lynn did, but expanding the roster of strong relationships will also be important.

Yet a third way of looking at resilience is to explore whether these children have some characteristic or trait that explains their resilience, something that other kids with similar early life adversity do not have. Is there some ultimately mysterious ability, despite long odds against it, to succeed in school, in relationships, in careers, and so on? Researchers have devoted quite a bit of time to seeking the essential components of resilience, and indeed, a couple of attributes have been linked to it. One is having a higher than average IQ. But despite recent efforts—most notably among cognitive neuroscientists—we have not yet seen specific interventions that work to raise IQs among children effectively or reliably. Another is grit, which psychologist Angela Duckworth identified in her book *Grit: The Power of Passion and Perseverance* as a characteristic that is as necessary to success as talent. Accessing the grit within, she says, is a matter of effort and determination. But this is yet to be studied in kids who have struggled through early adversity and may be carrying the burden of SDR as a result.

Most likely, kids who benefit from the opportunities provided by the ordinary magic of strong social connections at different times in development and with a range of people do so in part by acquiring new skills and competencies for characteristics like self-regulation and perseverance. Make no mistake: this is a challenging process, and it doesn't happen overnight. But it does happen.

This potential for resilience was borne out in a conversation I recently had with the principal of an alternative school for children who have fallen off the mainstream academic track. On a daily basis he confronted scores of students prone to the impulsivity, attention problems, and aggression characteristic of the SDR child. He was convinced, based on his experience, that all schools—not just his own—could create, as he put it, a strong "culture of resilience" that would allow them to thrive. While he believed that schools should continue to bring in solid, evidence-based educational and intervention programs, he also felt that they needed to bolster the relationship between teacher and student in order to help students who are struggling because they hadn't been fortunate enough to build the necessary emotional foundation at home. Teachers should establish trust, he explained, creating an authentic connection that makes students feel they matter.

He then told me a story of a student who'd been nearly

impossible to reach. The boy alternated between states of intense prickliness and complete withdrawal. He was not easy to teach and not easy to keep under control when he was in an aggressive phase. While most teachers would have sought to "let sleeping bears lie" and encourage withdrawal, this student's teacher took the time to learn about his interests, to talk regularly even at times when he was prickly. The teacher eventually turned their conversations toward how those passions might become goals and contribute to a plan for the future. This was a long process with a lot of personal investment. But the principal emphasized that the payoff could be enormous—as it was in this case. The student made enough of a personal connection to begin caring about rising to expectations, believing in the promise that the teacher made clear existed for him.

What struck me most about this story was how closely it aligned with the research on resilience—positive relationships offer restorative powers. And yet, it is important to note that, so far, analyzing the various studies that have looked at the long-term outcome for kids who have struggled early on, only a small minority are able to achieve the level of success that we would characterize as resilient. Therefore, it is imperative, as I will detail later, that we push for changes in social policy that will address the ways families can be better supported as well as make these relationships more accessible to those kids who are not born with—or into—more fortunate circumstances. Most especially, we need to figure out how to break the cycle of stress and social inequality that leads to far too many kids *needing* to overcome the odds in order to thrive. We can do much more to stack the odds in their favor to begin with.

Some Resources for Helping During the School Years

Laurie Grossman, *Master of Mindfulness: How to Be Your Own Super-hero in Times of Stress,* New Harbinger, 2016.

Kari Dunn-Buron, *When My Worries Get Too Big! A Relaxtion Book for Children Who Live with Anxiety*, AAPC Publishing, 2006

Daniel J. Siegel and Tina Payne Bryson, *The Whole-Brain Child: 12 Revolutionary Strategies to Nurture Your Child's Developing Mind*, Delacorte, 2011.

Daniel J. Siegel and Tina Payne Bryson, *The Whole-Brain Child Workbook: Practical Exercises, Worksheets and Activities to Nurture Developing Minds,* PESI, 2015.

Ross W. Greene, *Raising Human Beings: Creating a Collaborative Partnership with Your Child*, Scribner, 2016.

Tamar Chansky, *Freeing Your Child from Anxiety, Revised and Updated Edition: Practical Strategies to Overcome Fears, Worries, and Phobias and Be Prepared for Life—From Toddlers to Teens*, Harmony, 2014.

Katharina Manassis, *Keys to Parenting Your Anxious Child*, Barron's, 2015.

Carolyn Daitch and Lissah Lorberbaum, *The Road to Calm Workbook*, W. W. Norton, 2016.

Eline Snel and Jon Kabat-Zinn, *Sitting Still Like a Frog: Mindfulness Exercises for Kids (and Their Parents)*, Shambhala Publications, 2013.

4

ONTO THE STAGE:

Stress and Coping in Adolescence

BY THE TIME ADOLESCENCE ARRIVES, key foundations of later development have been set: stress physiology is mostly locked, behavioral habits are well established, and educational trajectories are largely grooved in. For kids who continue to show signs of SDR and haven't had the benefit of the kinds of interactions that lead to resilience, these patterns can seem beyond the possibility of change. Fortunately, adolescence is also a period in which there are profound physical changes that make new patterns possible. The adolescent brain undergoes more change than at any time since infancy—with a rapid growth of new brain cells and the building of brain circuits—and the physical and hormonal changes of puberty open the door for dynamic changes in established patterns. The changes that occur during this time also offer new opportunities for intervention, especially by engaging new capacities for self-reflection and identity, as well as through deeper social connections with peers. But for those who are struggling with how to adapt while trying to manage an amped-up stress system, it can be a path filled with risks as well as opportunities. The key is for parents, educators, and caregivers to help them to develop and make use of these new capabilities, in part by recognizing the particularly challenging path they face.

Up to this point, a child's epigenetic fate—in terms of his stress system, and the ways of dealing with that—have largely been shaped by other people. But this only remains so for as long as the child is dependent on his parents, teachers, or mentors for nurturance and support. Once he hits adolescence, roughly from twelve to twenty years old, he can navigate life with greater autonomy; this is true in many regards, but in relation to learning how to manage an amped-up stress system, this is an especially effective time. The basic changes that take place in the brain during this period allow for a more mature understanding of one's own drives and behavior. If the first critical period is when the stress response system is shaped in early childhood—when we lay the foundation for a lifetime— then the *second* critical period arrives in adolescence, when we are offered another chance to build on the strengths and shore up the weaknesses in that foundation. At this point, adolescents can, to a degree, take control of their own stress response system and manage it in the service of their own goals. Running alongside these favorable new circumstances, however, are new stressors, raising the stakes for stress-dysregulated kids. Familial relationships, of course, are still significant at this time, particularly as adolescents have only just begun to navigate this newfound level of awareness; parents remain valuable guides for their children, helping to take advantage of the potential changes they might make in their thought processes during this pivotal time.

THE TEEN BRAIN

Among the most important traits that distinguish humans from other animals is the ability for self-reflection, the ability to see oneself as being potentially able to control one's own thoughts, emotions, and actions. While other animals, such as apes and dolphins, possess components of this, our level of awareness extends much further. We are the only animals, for example, who can make detailed plans, collaboratively solve problems, and anticipate the future. These abilities are primarily based in our prefrontal cortex system (PFC), the so-called top brain. The PFC in human brains is more prominent than in any other animal—and it is a strikingly powerful tool.

The active development of this part of the brain during adolescence presents meaningful opportunities to manage stress. During this time, the PFC establishes our ability to control impulsive behavior—psychologists call it "inhibitory control"—as well as a whole new set of cognitive skills around planning, which provides a perspective on the future not available to younger children. There is also an improvement in rational analysis and logical thinking. This is critical as these new-found traits can be applied to the self, allowing for insights into one's own mind not possible prior to adolescence. This leads to greater self-awareness as well as the distinct shaping of an identity.

It's during this time that adolescents begin to think about what kind of person they want to be and what kinds of commitments they want to make—to ideals, religious beliefs, or passionate interests. During this time, the PFC also begins to establish pathways—specifically, synapses—to many other parts of the brain, gradually taking control of functions such as choosing one behavior over another and, important for our purposes, deciding what to react to. The PFC controls a range of executive functions, including regulating attention—being able to concentrate for long periods of time as well as multitasking—and expanding working memory, so that it's possible, for example, to complete multistep math and logic problems.

Simultaneously, however, the "bottom brain"—made up of the limbic system, whose primary task is to wire up the brain's circuitry for emotional arousal, sensation seeking, risk, and reward—is evolving even more rapidly in a way that makes it harder to step back from a situation to evaluate what it means for us, and how best to handle it. This part of the brain, at its peak at around age fourteen or fifteen, is associated with a host of typical adolescent behaviors and emotions: risk taking, impulsivity, sexual desire, and catastrophic thinking. Because the bottom brain's rate of growth outstrips the top brain's development at this time, the urges stemming from this part of the brain frequently take over. This is a time at which kids are typically taking risks, and not all of them good ones. The bottom brain wants to get out and try new things, to have exciting experiences—which, unfortunately, can include anything from reckless driving to skateboarding without a helmet to having unsafe sex—before the top brain, which offers better judgment and better decision making, has had a chance to catch up. If you have ever wondered why your teenager is all accelerator and no brakes, this is your answer.

There is a study that nicely illustrates the fierce competition that takes place between the top and bottom of a teenager's brain. Researchers asked people ranging in age from seven to twenty-seven years old to stare at a screen while undergoing an MRI. The participants were instructed to look in the opposite direction when a star came up on the screen—if, for example, the star came up on the right-hand corner, they were to look at the left-hand corner. Since the desire is to look where something is happening—we are, in fact, hardwired by evolution to do so—this is very difficult. When a group of seven- to nine-year-olds tried, they were unable to do it because the PFC, or top brain, has not matured at this point to have enough impulse control to overcome the automatic response. Most adolescents and adults, on the other hand, *are* able to do it, at least eventually. The PFC was extremely active during the learning phase in both groups; the top brain has to work very hard to control the impulse to look. Once the adults mastered the task, though, the top-brain activity leveled off and the activity shifted to the visual motor cortex—a likely example of the PFC system delegating the task. For adolescents, however, the PFC never steps down. It has to remain highly active the whole time in order to concentrate on the task at hand. If something else were to come along and tug at their attention—say, a friend joking and causing a commotion in the passenger seat of a car—the top brain would cede to the impulsivity of the bottom brain fairly easily. (This is why there is now a graduated driver's licensing system in most states that limits the number of unrelated minors allowed in the car with a newly licensed teen driver, along with other restrictions. It is, in fact, a highly effective policy, reducing serious accidents, including fatal ones, by about 50 percent.)

This tension between consciousness (top) and impulsivity (bottom) is further heightened by three major components of overall brain development at this time: *synaptogenesis*, which provides a major burst of new brain cells just at the beginning of adolescence; *synaptic pruning*, which selects which of those cells will survive and wire up specific neural circuits; and *myelination*, which speeds up connections between brain circuits. It's worth examining each of these more carefully to understand how they also subtly shape a teenager's behavior and future, and the opportunities they offer to help teens deal better with stress.

We used to think, not that long ago, that the rapid proliferation of new brain cells—synaptogenesis—was confined to the beginning of life and that we already had all the brain cells we were going to get by the end of early childhood. We now know that isn't the case: new brain cells are born throughout our lifetimes but never again at the pace we saw from conception to the end of the first year of life. This rapid acceleration in the birth of brain cells happens only once more, in early adolescence. Basically, this period of life offers a fresh round of neural material. Through a complicated process, that material is sculpted into new brain circuits that support thinking and behavior. How those circuits are built is shaped in large part by what the teen experiences.

HEBB'S LAW, OR WHAT FIRES TOGETHER WIRES TOGETHER

All these new brain cells provided by synaptogenesis don't do much unless they are put to work. This entails establishing and strengthening brain circuits, creating the habits that take form at this point. When a teen tries something new—for example, learning a tennis stroke—neurons (the cells that make up the brain circuits) in a particular circuit will fire. When this behavior is repeated, the neurons will begin to fire together more often; they will become wired together, which strengthens the skill. But this can work in the other direction—that is, the neurons and synapses not used will die off: this is synaptic pruning. This is a moment then when the brain listens to the environment, fine-tuning itself with respect to the circumstances it finds itself in.

For example, one kind of neuron that proliferates during this period is called a receptor cell, which is developed to respond to particular kinds of neurochemicals. One of these neurochemicals is dopamine—the pleasure detector, known as such because it tags a pleasurable activity as something to be remembered and to do again. So if a teen begins to really enjoy reading novels at this time, the more these receptors will "fire" in response to the behavior, and the stronger their links to this particular behavior will be. This neural pathway, in turn, will become a well-worn groove in the teen's mind—and reading will become something that she will want to do more and more in her spare time.

But this process doesn't always produce such a positive effect. Take, for instance, nicotine receptors—so named because they literally seek signs of this stimulant in the brain; if these receptors are exposed to nicotine in a person before the age of about fifteen or sixteen, they will not die off but will instead start lighting up, firing and wiring together, and remaining active. If nicotine is not found, however, most of these receptors will die off, no longer "asking" for the stimulant. But even modest use (less than a pack of cigarettes per week for a couple of months) can keep these receptors alive, strengthening the desire for more nicotine, and sharply raising the chance of addiction. The effects of other kinds of repetitive activity are harder to pin down, because they likely have multiple effects. Take video game play, which is a frequent activity among many teens. Some argue that it wires up a penchant for violent acting out (in first-person-shooter games, for example), whereas others argue that teens make the distinction between real and imaginary, and that the real effect is to enhance the rapid thinking-to-motor-coordination that enhances the use of modern technology. The behavioral evidence for one or the other side of this debate—and both could be true—is nonexistent at the level of brain circuitry at this time.

Myelination is another process that starts going faster in adolescence than at any other time of life. It involves a speeding up of connections among different brain circuits by way of a thin layer of fatty tissue called myelin. When this coats the circuits, messages can travel more quickly through them. If Hebb's Law builds the pathways of the brain, myelination makes them more like highways. Any new skill or habit that an adolescent is trying out at this time—piano, skiing or, less favorably, drinking—is going to be acquired more quickly than at any other time in life. Myelination also contributes to a behavior becoming a habit—signals travel so quickly and efficiently down myelinated pathways that whatever you are doing can start to feel like second nature, almost without conscious thought.

BRAIN REVOLUTION: FOR BETTER OR WORSE

Given the enormous number of changes happening in the brain—and the tug of war between reason and desire occurring simultaneously—this can be a tricky period to navigate. The good news is, even for a teen with SDR, there is great potential for learned behavior and habits that will help to set a better, calmer course, emotionally speaking. The biggest advantage that materializes at this time is the ability to appraise one's own emotions—particularly when stress kicks in—and learning to separate real alarms from false ones. That is, your body might be telling you something but it isn't necessarily giving you the full story. At this point, under certain circumstances, adolescents can step back and evaluate what is really going on for them.

As it happens, there are actually two slightly different brain circuits that can activate fear arousal and the reactive stress response that follows. Just like we have fast-twitch and slow-twitch muscles in the body—think of a sprint versus a marathon—we also have two ways in which to get the stress response moving. Although both neural pathways are traveled quickly, there are essential differences. The first route is automatic, and largely hardwired. Some stimuli appear to be natural fear inducers: a snake for most of us, for example, or the shadow of a hawk for a rodent in a field.

When we come upon one of these natural fear inducers, the perception goes straight to the amygdala, our primary brain circuit for a fear response. In short order, it signals the HPA axis to launch into action. This happens automatically—and our brains are hardwired to do so—because the longer it takes to get going, the more likely we are at risk for not surviving the encounter. This is the stress equivalent of a fast-twitch muscle.

Another aspect of normal adolescent development carries special risks for SDR teens. Possibly because of the hormonal changes that come along with puberty, the stress response system is even more active for everyone. Cortisol release to experimentally induced stress increases with the onset of puberty—perhaps as an evolved protective function for teens as they start exploring the world outside the orbit of their family and group. But since the SDR teen is already more amped-up, this is a further amplification that magnifies the problem.

There are plenty of other situations not programmed into our evolutionary response that can lead to stress, particularly in adolescence: feeling you've been snubbed by your crush at school, a fight with a friend, doing badly on a quiz. These—our slow-twitch stress reactions—typically have an intermediate step in the brain circuitry. And we are able to take advantage of that extra time to conduct a cognitive appraisal: "Is this something I should truly feel anxious about? Is there another way to react to this?"

It is possible to consciously acquire this keen awareness of our instincts and the propensity to judge whether our fears are worthy—this is a function of the PFC, after all. And it is precisely what mindfulness training aims to do. The core idea of mindfulness is that through training and practice we can become more fully aware of what we are experiencing in any given moment and can learn to direct and guide our reactions rather than to be ruled by them through our automatic responses. Mindfulness has evolved into a broad category of approaches to therapy for stress reduction, alleviating depression, and other psychological conditions or disorders (like borderline personality disorder).

Mindfulness can be taught formally by a teacher or therapist, but it can also be informally supported by a parent. Parents can also demonstrate appropriate behavior. As parents, you don't need to jump in when your teens are exhibiting a stress reaction or begin to stress along with them when they are overreacting; you can lead the way by stepping back and inquiring calmly about what is worrying your teen. Learning to self-assess in this way doesn't, incidentally, mean that the stress system is less of an annoyance, but there is greater potential to control it. And the longer and more effectively this is practiced, the more new neurons will develop—firing and wiring together—to sustain this skill. Eventually this can replace an old habit of immediately reacting with anxiety by essentially providing an emotional pause button, allowing the teenager to stop and see things differently. (Meanwhile, the process of myelination means this will be practiced with increasing dexterity.)

And yet, just as the bottom brain can override the top, this opportunity to reflect can be turned against oneself in a way that *provokes* the stress system. Think of the teen who feels she's been slighted by a friend in school—the friend brushed by her without saying hello after class. Later that night, chatting or texting with friends or just thinking about it on her own, she goes over it in great detail, analyzing it from every angle. She can easily call to mind many ways that this could get worse in the days to come and may spend considerable time trying to play out various scenarios: "Maybe she's so mad at me that she'll turn everyone else against me or start a bunch of nasty rumors." The end points of these future scenarios are likely to be painful to contemplate.

Of course, she may have completely misread her friend, who may have been late for a meeting or distracted by her own problems—but that's not what matters to her. What matters is the potential social cost, and that is what occupies her attention and her emotions. You've probably experienced this kind of rumination yourself, or at least seen it in others, and it has effects far beyond the bad mood it brings on. It's stressful, to say the least. Thinking negatively about how things are going in life or obsessing about things that went wrong earlier in the day or about worrisome possibilities looming in the near future, any of these can spark a fearful or anxious thought, and then it's off to the races for the stress response system. Even if nothing actually happened to set it off—if it was simply an imagined or recalled event—the HPA axis reacts in the same way regardless of the source. Many SDR teens will also have hostile attribution bias, meaning they are more likely to perceive fantasy slights. And because this will largely operate through the automatic fast-twitch route to setting off the stress system, bouts of this kind of negative thinking may become self-sustaining. Building in a mindful slow-twitch pause button makes it possible to avoid activating the stress response.

In addition to generating excess stress, which of course carries risks, this kind of rumination can also raise nighttime cortisol—almost surely interfering with a good night's sleep. And because adolescents have the ability to override sleep signals, whereas children generally do not, this can carry on well into the early morning hours. Sleep deficits take a toll on everyone, but especially on teens. They need more sleep than adults—and perhaps even more than children a bit younger than them—because of the energy demands of rapid physical growth. They also have a delayed sleep phase, for physiological reasons, drifting toward the night owl end of the dimension. This, combined with generally early high school start times, contributes to even bigger sleep deficits. When these sleep deficits pile up, they can cause a vicious cycle because sleep deficits lead to poorer self-regulation, greater difficulty in managing social interactions, and significant decreases in attention and learning.

JANICE, LONNIE, AND EARL

When Lonnie and Earl, parents of three children, first met with another colleague of mine, they were nearing the end of their patience with their daughter Janice. She was in the spring of ninth grade and had been suspended after marijuana was found in her locker (she admitted it was hers). Her parents were beyond worried because of her frequently withdrawn and sullen attitude and her desire to spend all her time with a crowd from school who engaged in high-risk behavior.

They were also mystified, because all of this seemed so out of character for her. She had never been in trouble at school and had been close with her family, which included two other children, twin boys in the third grade. But as my colleague drew out the parents, another story emerged. Janice had recently faced a number of major transitions. Just before ninth grade, the family had moved from Detroit to Atlanta, so her father, who had completed his career in the army, could start his new career. Beyond the move itself, many other supports and expectations that Janice had were uprooted. Her circle of friends back home was not right at hand, and although she kept in close touch by social media, seeing all the connections and fun at long distance often made her feel worse rather than better. And although she was not unfamiliar with racism as a young African American teen growing up in Detroit, it had not been as central a defining characteristic in her mind before the move down South. Her middle school had been relatively small, and she had enjoyed success on the school's soccer team. But at the new, quite large high school in Atlanta, she wasn't competitive enough to make the team; unlike her, many of the students had the advantage of multiple years of club soccer and travel teams. She found it difficult to fit in at school academically, struggling to get Bs when she had regularly had As before, as well as socially, where she quickly became sensitive to peer rejection, both real and perceived.

Her parents described her as doing well at school before, although they did relate a history of Janice being quick to react to slights and unwilling to adapt to new situations. But they had maintained strong control over her behavior, especially her father, who brooked no deviation from the rules he laid down.

This strong parental involvement had worked in the past to keep her on a productive path. After the move, her father was deeply involved in establishing his new career. Her mother, Lonnie, was working part-time and focusing on her younger twin brothers, who were also having trouble adjusting to the move. Janice often retreated to her room, spending time on social media, both with her old friends but also in anonymous chat rooms with a different group of kids than she had been used to. She felt rejected at school and tended to isolate herself there as well. On the occasions when Lonnie tried to connect with her, Janice interpreted it as checking up on her and blaming her for things not going well. She thought the blame fell more on her parents.

As she wandered around at lunch breaks and other times on her own at school, Janice connected with a crowd that was equally disengaged from school. They introduced her to alcohol and marijuana, which did offer temporary relief from her anxiety and anger. Her hair-trigger temper, hypersensitivity, and tendency to see hostile intent in other teens got in the way of her connecting with kids who were doing well. After her suspension, Lonnie tried to break the cycle by arranging home schooling for her, but Janice was just as unwilling to do the work for the online, virtual classrooms as she had been at regular school.

My colleague discerned that Janice did have some real vulnerability around managing stress, making it unusually difficult for her to deal with new and challenging situations. What was paramount was to find a way for her to reengage with other kids who were on a more positive developmental path and to work on some mindfulness skills that would help her to understand and make more accurate appraisals of her own situation and responses.

It took quite some time to overcome Janice's barriers. In working to find out what might connect with her, it came to light that she was deeply fond of animals. With some gentle prodding, she agreed to look into a volunteer opportunity at a local animal shelter. There, she met with a small group of teen volunteers who shared her passion. Eventually, Lonnie allowed her to bring home a rescue puppy, for which Janice had been lobbying. Along with ongoing therapy to ingrain new habits, Janice showed significant improvement.

When she returned to school for the start of tenth grade, Janice had a few good friends, a renewed sense of purpose, and a new sense of mastery after acquiring skills at the animal shelter. Although her parents continued to keep a close eye on her, she made use of these skills and interests to get back on a more promising path.

FRIENDSHIP: BOON OR BANE?

Despite the seeming minefield of complexities related to social life in adolescence—which are a genuine source of concern—truly close friendships can actually bring about some of the same effects as the most devoted parenting in infancy. Just as there is a second chance offered to kids at school—through a warm and attentive teacher or mentor—the same transformation can take place now with a close friend or romantic attachment. Most especially, a supportive, close relationship helps adolescents to reduce stress, both through social support and biologically, offering oxytocin and serotonin as a counterforce to excess cortisol. Interestingly, a good friend can also provide the basis for seeing oneself or one's circumstances in a different light; this creates another way to learn how to appraise situations and oneself more realistically and to put in place the "pause to reflect" strategy. Say, for instance, a teen with SDR, along with her good friend, encounters a group of other kids. Afterward, this teen reports that she was given the cold shoulder by someone in the group—but her friend doesn't see it that way at all. "I don't think he was dissing you," her friend explains. "He said 'hi' and then he got distracted." This is a revelatory counterpoint and, over time, this fresh perspective can go a long way toward modifying a stress reaction.

Over the course of adolescence, the nature of these interactions undergoes a shift, as puberty works its magic. One of the effects of this change is that it signals potential availability for romantic involvements—puberty takes a child and produces an adult. How developmentally ready any given teen is for romantic involvement should not be judged by outward appearances, but if the time is right, this is another connection that carries with it the potential to alter the behavior of an adolescent with an amped-up stress system.

In fact, among the surrogate relationships that can help reshape how a teen approaches the world of social connections and emotional self-regulation, an intimate relationship with a peer is one of the most powerful. This is not about sex but about intimacy—when a true sense of trust and openness is fostered. In a study conducted in the 1990s, researchers looked at kids struggling with aggression issues at age fifteen to sixteen years old and then continued to follow them for a ten-year period. A strong characteristic of those who were doing better at the end of that decade—judged by school achievement, work history, and positive interpersonal relationships—was having had a fulfilling romantic relationship, one that lasted at least a couple of years, during that decade-long span.

It must be said that aspects of these relationships—both friendships and romantic attachments—are far more difficult for SDR teens. When there is a negative reaction of any sort, as typically crop up in any teen relationship, the defensive fight-or-flight reaction is likely to be triggered. Once triggered, it can lead to behavior that will be ever more isolating. A hair-trigger fight response is likely to lead to social rejection, as peers won't want to bother with someone whose behavior is hard to predict or even possibly dangerous. This reactive kind of aggression is a major risk for developing good relationships. It's important to note that not all aggressive behavior is the same, though. Instrumental aggression, getting others to do what you want, is somewhat paradoxically an occasional boost to popularity, conferring higher social status

The flight response, by contrast, is usually manifested as withdrawing from or avoiding social interactions altogether. This can be a precarious negotiation for parents—not to mention difficult to watch—as teens need to learn to navigate their own relationships at this point. Where parents could once step in and try to fix things, the aim now is to leave room for the teenager to steer his or her own course while also maintaining enough of an emotional connection so that there is still a sense of foundation.

A DIFFERENT KIND OF INDEPENDENCE

At the same time that parents begin to step back, the atmosphere of school changes rather dramatically, too. The relatively more nurturing, family-like organization of elementary education gives way to a more explicitly competitive environment, where it's clear adolescents are expected to rely more on themselves. The message from teachers and the system becomes much more about judgment than comfort: you will have assignments with deadlines, you'll be competing with fellow students, you'll be graded on everything. This is made to feel even more high stakes by the realization that school success is critical to career success, especially in the intense atmosphere of social inequality—a topic we'll come back to in later chapters.

For teens struggling with a disrupted stress system, this may be something of a tipping point. This transition happens when many kids, even those not struggling with high stress levels, are not quite ready for it, when their PFC-based planning capabilities are still immature. And, because many SDR kids tend to be impulsive, and thus put more strain on the PFC, more of them will be caught in this mismatch of emotional readiness and the stark demands of middle and high school.

The same requirements raised in Chapter 3 remain true of school at this stage: teachers need to communicate to students that they matter, and that being part of the community is important. When students believe their social connections are authentic, that they are valued, then they are much more open to a wide range of life lessons. One of the consequences of establishing a meaningful relation between students and teachers—and using it to support healthy development—is that students remain truly engaged in schooling; they are not just putting in the time.

There has been much research recently looking at the characteristics of school systems that have begun to carry out this redesign most effectively. These creative efforts are still in process, but we can already begin to see the outline of some key features that work. One finding that illustrates a key to bolstering enthusiasm is that if kids are engaged in at least one activity in school outside of academics—whether that is a sports team, a drama club, or an arts class—this essentially reinforces a bond with the school. In these cases, the most at-risk students, as compared to others who don't have a connection to school outside of academics, are much more likely to excel as students and graduate from high school.

In addition to what parents can do directly to support a child or teen with SDR—continuing with an authoritative style of warm responsiveness combined with clear expectations; supporting a more self-aware, mindful approach to evaluating the teen's experiences; and remaining invested in a close emotional connection—there is the delicate dance that is important as a teen enters the larger world in a more independent way. Many parents are tempted to become overinvolved with how their teen is navigating the very difficult challenges that peers and school now present to them. For parents of a child with SDR, the desire to guide those interactions so as to protect their young teenager, it is even harder to take a step back and let them develop the skills they will need for the rest of their lives. On the other hand, this does not mean abandoning them to work it out on their own with little support. This push-pull is hard on both parents and teens, but maintaining lines of communication and modeling more mindful coping skills do help, even when the ride gets bumpy.

A climate of acceptance and adult investment in success creates an atmosphere in which adolescents can begin to build their identities within the context of an inclusive community. This will also hopefully allow for the discovery of a self that is no longer trapped in one's own childhood history.

Some Resources for Troubled Teens

Lisa M. Schab, *The Anxiety Workbook for Teens: Activities to Help You Deal with Anxiety and Worry*, New Harbinger, 2008

Christopher Willard, *Mindfulness for Teen Anxiety: A Workbook for Overcoming Anxiety at Home, at School, and Everywhere Else*, New Harbinger, 2014.

Mark C. Purcell and Jason R. Murphy, *Mindfulness for Teen Agers: A Workbook to Overcome Anger and Aggression Using MBSR and DBT Skills*, New Harbinger, 2014.

Sheri Van Dijk, *Don't Let Your Emotions Run Your Life for Teens: Dialectical Behavior Therapy Skills for Helping You Manage Mood Swings, Control Angry Outbursts, and Get Along with Others*, New Harbinger, 2011.

5

THE STRESS TESTS OF ADULTHOOD:

Managing Family, Work, and Relationships

STRESS-DYSREGULATED ADULTS, PARTICULARLY THOSE WHO haven't had the benefit of earlier supports that might have led to greater resilience, are often a burden to themselves and to others. Their sensitivity to slights, lack of trust, and tendency toward outbursts and withdrawal make them a minefield many would prefer to avoid. Their relationships in their families and their workplaces typically suffer because of this, generating negative responses in turn, further accelerating the stress cycle. This sometimes shows up at home or at work, or both, as *stress contagion,* as they pass along their heightened stress even to those with more typical stress response systems. As more individuals experience the kinds of early adversity that lead to SDR, the more ambient stress there is in many different day-to-day settings. This has contributed to a stress epidemic in our modern high-stress world, showing up in a raft of stress-related diseases and conditions that are on the rise including metabolic disorders like diabetes and cardiovascular disease, sleep disorders, and mental health issues like depression. SDR adults are at the highest risk for all of them.

But even if you or someone you love has made it to adulthood without addressing their SDR, there are ways to break the cycle, employing the same kinds of stress reducers we have seen before, but now with a greater possibility of making a self-directed choice to pursue them. The mitigating influence of building on strong social connections, and the conscious work-around of a mindful perspective on one's own life are prominent. These changes are not necessarily easy for the SDR adult, but they are possible and effective. Adults can come to understand, on their own and with encouragement from loved ones, that the stakes are high for their future health and well-being.

Up to this point, we have seen the ways in which a disrupted stress system affects a young person, but what can be done if you suspect an adult is grappling with this problem? Many people have approached me with just this question, wondering how they might know if this is the case or, more often, worrying it's too late; they or someone close to them must live out an inescapable fate. But that is not the case. As is true with every stage of stress dysregulation, knowing how it might be expressed and understanding what can be done to minimize the emotional burden—for the person struggling as well as for those around them—can make a difference. Merely recognizing that there is a reason for such behavior often offers some degree of relief.

WHAT DOES ADULT STRESS DYSREGULATION LOOK LIKE?

In many ways, an amped-up stress system in an adult resembles a more sophisticated version of its expression in teenagers. It invokes the same emotions but with slightly different behaviors. The adult version of rumination, for example, is often to obsess over problems at work or in relationships. Hostile attribution bias often shows up: the kids who were convinced they were purposefully bumped in the line prefigure the adults who are quick to perceive that their boss is giving them the cold shoulder or their girlfriend isn't being responsive. A too-stressed adult might continuously check e-mails late into the night, either seeking further evidence of a challenge or distracting themselves from their obsessions. (And, as with an adolescent, this kind of late-night screen activity also disrupts the diurnal system, which oversees the daily fluctuations of cortisol and goes into overdrive when there is too much stimulation at the time when it should be quieting down.) This same stressed adult might remember late at night that he forgot to send a work memo, and rather than reasonably decide that it can be done the following morning, he will escalate into catastrophic thinking—*The memo has to go out now. I'll be seen as not getting the job done. I could get fired.* This line of thinking will ramp higher and higher, flooding the body with more and more cortisol, making it that much harder to calm down again.

And yet straightforward anxiety is not the only way that SDR is communicated. It can also be expressed as anger; in fact, the two share a lot of the same brain circuitry and physiology, specifically the link from the bottom brain to the stress response system. This reaction also harkens back to Steve Suomi's monkeys from Chapter 1, the ones raised without mothers, who didn't know how to stop play fighting. They'd get into a light tussle and then the SDR monkeys would rapidly escalate to real aggression, continuing to pound on their mate even after he had curled into a defenseless ball; or they would provoke a strong retaliation from their victim or his relatives and allies. Similarly, adults who channel their stress through anger are quick to react when things are not going their way. Their tempers rise immediately—and then they find it difficult to come back down because their system is urging them to keep fighting. Plus, anger often provides temporary control of their environment.

This kind of runaway train of anger is most notable when there is nobody there to put an end to it. With the monkeys, fights are often stopped by the mother of the young victim; she will swat her child's aggressor away or even deliver her own blows. Among humans, there are other interventions: an adult can defend himself against a verbal or physical attack or a superior will interfere with such episodes. But if those constraints are absent, it can be hard for the SDR adult to get control of himself; think of the boss who explodes over minor issues and is unable to let them go even after proper acknowledgment.

This spike in cortisol and its subsequent unremitting flow can be turned inward, too, translating into a feeling of agitation, where everything seems to overwhelm, there is too much coming in, and the person feels unable to handle it all at once. This can also develop into the flight response, when someone shuts down entirely, unable to think about the overpowering circumstances; in this case, a person will basically retreat to a corner, burying her head in her hands. The flight response can take a person so far off the track that she loses the ability to wind back up again or get excited. In such a person, the "up" regulation of the system, which involves the healthy discharge of cortisol and urges us to get back into the game, to push ourselves to fulfill goals and ambitions, is disrupted. There is also a strong link between SDR and depression. If stress dysregulation is expressed through depression in adolescence, for example, this is a strong indication there will be subsequent episodes throughout life when there are stress triggers.

JULIE, PETER, AND BEN

When Julie brought her three-year-old, Ben, to an autism specialist, a colleague of mine, for an evaluation, she was clearly quite distressed. Her husband Peter was unable to join them because it interfered with his standard eighty-hour workweek, which he hewed to religiously in hopes of finally becoming a partner in a prestigious law firm. The detailed autism diagnostic interview, though, revealed deeper reasons for Julie's obvious agitation and anxiety, beyond her fears for Ben.

She reported having been highly anxious from time to time throughout her life, responding badly when things became difficult, like being dumped by a fiancé a few weeks before a planned wedding. When she met Peter not long afterward, she was attracted to his calm, unflappable demeanor and didn't miss the tension of her earlier stormy relationship, in which she often felt off-kilter and agitated. Peter's style was like a balm to her, smoothing out the edges and helping her stay on an even keel.

She had a difficult pregnancy and birth with Ben, including several significant flu and illness episodes. Not long after Ben was born, she began to have significant worries about him. He was hard to soothe and didn't respond well to being held and cuddled. He seemed to prefer being left alone in his crib for extended periods. In the mother-baby groups she joined, she noticed that Ben was much less likely to attend to others, either babies or their parents. When she expressed these concerns to Peter, he attributed them to her history of anxiety, which she experienced as dismissive. Both sets of grandparents—Ben was the first grandchild on both sides—lived nearby, and they also assured her that Ben was going to be just fine: some babies are just different. At an eighteen-month well-baby visit to her pediatrician, Ben's behavior was not unusual enough to trigger his concern. As Julie experienced no validation from anyone about her concerns, she began to worry that perhaps it was all in her head; this only increased her anxiety and agitation.

By the time he was twenty-four months old, Ben's language was lagging behind and his low level of social engagement was becoming even clearer to Julie. He often responded with irritation to her social bids, not liking to be intruded on. At a thirty-month checkup, the pediatrician was not greatly concerned, but suggested that it would be appropriate to get an evaluation, if only to ease Julie's mind. However, she learned that in her area there would be up to a two-year delay in getting a formal evaluation. Peter and the rest of the family continued to dismiss her concerns and to criticize her for her "obsession." But, she reported, she was the one who was with Ben all the time, and she knew that something wasn't right.

When a cancellation opened up a slot for Ben six months later, she jumped at the chance. After a detailed evaluation, my colleague informed Julie that Ben was definitely on the autism spectrum. She responded with a rush of emotions that was almost overwhelming: validation that she hadn't been imagining it, fear about Ben's future, worry about how she could handle a child with ASD, and anger at Peter and her family for dismissing her concerns for so long. When she learned that the best intervention for Ben was applied behavior analysis, she was encouraged that help could be available but also terrified that she would need to become deeply involved in helping to deliver this intensive program. She expected that it would fall only on her, as Peter's calmness morphed into distance from her and Ben when he learned of the diagnosis, and its implications.

The specialist strongly recommended that Julie also seek therapy for herself, to help her deal with the feelings from having carried this load by herself for so long and to provide support as she tried to navigate this new world that, she learned, would involve constant interaction with agencies and then schools, many of which were not well equipped to work with kids like Ben. Her anxiety and agitation would go sky-high when Ben would act out at family gatherings and in public, when she could almost feel the disdain directed at her for being unable to manage his behavior. She could see that the brief interlude of calm when she and Peter got together was the exception, and that she wasn't sure how she would cope with this new, major stress, which had set her back on the path of fear and anxiety that threatened to overwhelm her.

In addition to emotional and behavioral overload, hardship can trigger an amped-up stress response for those who suffer with SDR, and this recurrence throughout life can manifest physically in adulthood, too—as was hinted at with Michael Marmot's study of lower-ranking British civil servants who were four times as likely to suffer serious illness than those in higher-ranking administrative positions. This study, in fact, paved the way for what has since become known in psychology and health research as the "allostatic load," a term introduced by Bruce McEwen, a neuroscientist who has been a pioneer in this field of research over the last four decades. The allostatic load refers to the physical toll taken on the body over time when someone experiences repeated or chronic stress. When the stress system is called on too often, the short-term boost from cortisol activation accumulates, producing more of this hormone than is actually needed. Because excess cortisol is toxic to most organs, there are a number of negative health consequences. Studies have repeatedly shown a clear association between excess cortisol and metabolic syndromes such as obesity and diabetes, as well as sleep disorders and cardiovascular disease.

IS IT TOO LATE TO CHANGE?

By the time we reach adulthood, our patterns of behavior and the ways we respond emotionally—including the triggers and coping mechanisms of the stress response system—are more or less established. The days of being able to change in a relatively easy or flexible way have passed by this point. But there is still a chance of modification with enough awareness and effort; though it is harder to achieve change in adulthood, things are not set in stone.

As we saw in Chapter 4, during the critical periods when change is relatively easier to achieve—in infancy and again in adolescence—there is major growth in the number of brain cells being created. This process, synaptogenesis, allows the brain to create new circuitry as it adapts to external circumstances. Synaptogenesis, however, does not end with adolescence; it continues throughout life, even well into old age, albeit at a slower pace.

So rewiring is indeed possible at later stages of life. To do so, however, newer circuits will have to compete against well-established ones, which already have a well-grooved dynamic system. These circuits have the characteristic of dynamic systems known as "attractor states," meaning many different pieces of the system can reel us back in if we try to escape. Recent brain imaging of depression, for example, makes clear that many different aspects of the brain are involved in major episodes: how we think about things, how we feel about things, how we get motivated to do things. These aspects also appear to be so tightly linked that when one lights up, it quickly spreads to the other areas. A negative thought can activate a negative feeling, which can lead to a temporary lack of motivation.

If someone has long expressed stress through anger, a similar cascade occurs. This will light up all the familiar circuits leading to destructive behavior. Until another behavior is engaged for long enough to create a competing circuit, then it will be difficult to stray from this attractor state—in this case, an explosion of rage. For the SDR adult in particular, these circuits have been firing together for so long that they are that much harder to adjust.

And yet new skills that come with maturity can be tapped to make the kind of constructive changes that allow for healthier circuits to be forged in the brain. The first is a greater capacity for self-knowledge. By this time, we have had many opportunities to see what has and hasn't worked for us, and if we are open to seeing these clearly, we can fine-tune our behaviors with our best interests in mind. This is the essence of mindfulness—paying attention and acting with purpose and an informed sense of oneself. For instance, if a person with a high tendency toward stress feels tied up in knots over a work problem but is also conscious of his own amped-up stress system, he will know to take the time to break his dilemma down, sorting out a practical solution or at least creating a plan to move toward one. The problem may not be immediately solved, but simply acting on it can help to abate anxiety. Perhaps he will need to clear his head first and realizes that taking a walk or a run would be a good way to do that. Physical activity, in fact, burns off a good deal of cortisol, allowing for a clearer perspective. Even better, the person might connect with a friend to exercise, which gives the double benefit of energy expenditure and social connection.

Along with conscious mindfulness, social connection provides a strong opportunity to spur change in both the brain and behavior. Remember that the two feel-good social neurohormones, serotonin and oxytocin, counteract excess cortisol. So developing habits that put a priority on seeking out positive social interactions, especially when stressed, is another way that a degree of brain rewiring is achievable. And while these shifts help with our thinking, feeling, and behavior, it is also important to realize they have a significant impact on physical health.

But this is not the end of the story. Perhaps the most difficult step is committing to changes for the long term. In part, this is so challenging because the default option for most adults struggling with SDR—or stress in general—is to take the quickest, least effortful, automatic route toward comfort. We all, in fact, have two different ways of thinking. One is this more automatic mode, while the other is a more effortful, conscious, analytic mode. (Cognitive scientists use the term "dual process model" for these two trains of thought. Nobel laureate Daniel Kahneman describes them as System 1 and System 2 in his bestselling book *Thinking Fast and Slow*.)

Unfortunately, adults often fall back on the quick-fix mode of dealing with stress. One thing many do is turn repeatedly to food. This habit can begin very early on, when babies become quickly dependent on sucrose as a way to soothe their emotions, a positive instinctual preference given that it counteracts cortisol. This impulse remains throughout life, however, driving people toward high-sugar, high-calorie foods as a quick fix for stress. (Later, we'll see how this occurs across the population, contributing to the obesity epidemic.) Another fast track to relieving stress is drinking or taking drugs, both of which offer an immediate but short-lived reprieve. All of these habits, of course, pose longer-term risks like obesity and addiction.

Lastly, SDR itself is a major disruptor of our efforts to change. At nearly every step, there are opportunities for the stress response to be triggered, leading a person away from the direction he consciously wants to go, and back into the very stress that he has been feverishly trying to escape.

Retraining our habits—and minds—therefore takes the adamant discipline required of any expertise; mastery follows effortful practice. Like an alcoholic trying to stay sober, stress management must be considered a lifetime issue. But it's also true that if you begin to make mindful choices as a habit—as well as develop relationships for support—the likelihood of making impulsive or destructive choices will diminish.

AGNES

Recently, a psychologist colleague of mine told me about a woman she'd been seeing as a patient. I'll call her Agnes; she is in her seventies and offers a portrait of what real change can look like when high stress has overtaken your life.

Agnes's current life is in many ways enviable. She is a successful academic in a small college town in New England where she lives with her husband of forty-seven years and where she raised her two children, a son and a daughter. Her children are adults now and live elsewhere, both having embarked on promising careers of their own. Agnes is also known in her community for having formed a distinguished performance collective, which assembles trios and quartets and arranges public performances. Agnes herself took up the viola in her forties and is also well regarded locally as a gifted amateur musician.

By the time she came to see my colleague, late in her life, Agnes had already been managing depressive episodes with therapy and psychopharmacological medication for several decades. So she was startled to have unexpectedly begun to experience a frequent sense of agitation as well as periodic panic attacks, when external pressures had gone down. This was something different from her longstanding battle with depression, which usually left her feeling low on energy and hope. Agnes was self-aware enough by this point to know that she might achieve some peace if she could explore, and hopefully pinpoint, what was riling her emotionally.

As her life story emerged in fits and starts over the course of many sessions, my friend learned that Agnes had had a significantly difficult childhood. When she was a baby, just a few months old, her father was killed in an industrial accident, leaving virtually no estate for her mother. And Agnes's own mother had been orphaned as a child. After the death of her husband, she decided that her daughter would be better off if raised by two parents. So before Agnes had even turned a year old, she'd been sent to a foster family in the same midwestern town as her mother. Agnes was provided for, but the family ethos was one of orderliness and restraint. The foster father, a businessman, felt his children should be raised with a forward marching sense of discipline—which also translated as a lack of emotional warmth. Meanwhile, Agnes's birth mother still wanted to see her occasionally, so she would appear for an afternoon every few months throughout Agnes's childhood, sweeping her daughter away for a glamorous afternoon and then delivering her back to her emotionally distant foster family.

This turbulent upbringing, however, didn't hold Agnes back from establishing herself in her career and raising a family of her own. In fact, it had propelled her, in that she consciously decided that she would find happiness in a life of her own choosing in adulthood. For years, Agnes focused her effort and attention on those goals. Now, as she grasped at why she might be feeling so anxious, she wondered if the winding down of her career and the success of her adult children, with their diminishing need for support, might be part of the problem. My colleague felt this might be true, but she felt that there was also something deeper rousing Agnes's anxieties.

Agnes, she came to realize, had developed such effective coping mechanisms to fend off the burdens of her early life—with a strong community and family as well as striving to achieve in her career—that she hadn't yet experienced the full range of her emotions. Along with managing her recurring depression, she had also suffered multiple physical ailments, especially diabetes and early symptoms of progressive heart disease. She acknowledged an ongoing problem with self-care with regard to these physical health issues but believed that it was something she just couldn't fit into her busy life.

She'd dealt with her childhood difficulties to a degree—particularly while exploring her depression in therapy—but it is possible for an inundated stress response system to find new forms of expression. Even when someone is capable of subduing SDR, as Agnes seemed to have done, this doesn't mean that it won't surface eventually, particularly as the circumstances that support coping mechanisms change. In Agnes's case, this shift came with advancing age, which gave her less of a sense of being carried along the current of her own expectations of family life and career. She also noted that her lack of attention to her physical health continued unabated, though she now had ample time to take care of herself.

Agnes, in therapy with my colleague, was able to take the time to reflect more on what her childhood had actually felt like. She came to understand that her highly disrupted attachment to her mother and the aloof atmosphere of her foster family's household were also playing a role in her sudden feelings of disconnection. As she brought this into view, her stress began to feel more manageable, but she also had to redirect her efforts in order to keep it from overwhelming her occasionally. She is still in therapy, for example, and has increased the time she spends with her musical community, since that gives her such pleasure and playing her viola allows her an escape. And though Agnes feels she is more successful on some days than others, she has fundamentally created a new system for handling her new and difficult emotions.

IN RELATION TO STRESS

When Sigmund Freud was reportedly asked what is at the core of a healthy life, he answered simply: "Lieben und arbeiten." To love and to work. To do both well is the great opportunity, and challenge, of a satisfying life. In both areas, the exceedingly stressed will come up against particular hurdles, but it is possible to find ways over or around them.

To Love

It might seem impossible for those with an overburdened stress system to have a relationship—given the descriptions of anxiety and anger and disengagement that can go along with it—but as fraught as their temperaments can be, these people can have many other appealing characteristics as well. In fact, many desirable traits easily live side by side with SDR: kindness, humor, charm, compassion, honesty, ambition, and generosity, among them. People with challenged stress systems can be excellent, albeit trying, partners.

And yet it is helpful if such relationships are entered into with eyes wide open. It's not easy to know whether someone is actually physiologically stress-dysregulated: there have been a handful of tests for stress methylation that have been conducted in experimental capacities, but a conclusive diagnosis remains elusive in everyday life. But even if SDR may not announce itself in an overt way, it is possible to detect a general pattern over time. In the heady early days of a relationship, we may well overlook behaviors that will become troublesome over the course of a long relationship. These behaviors might not even appear at the beginning. Since serotonin and oxytocin act as counterforces to cortisol—and both of these hormones surge in the early days of romance—hints of SDR may be subdued at this time. It may only be later, when the going gets tough, or when things become simply mundane, that the stress triggers begin to fire, prompting the challenges that come with the territory. In fact, what may later come across as endless agitation or off-key behavior may seem in the early days like high energy or an unconventional charm.

Later, with the daily hassles of collaborating, especially when each partner may have their own particular ideas of how things should be done, the stress response system can escalate quickly. And it is often the daily hassles, rather than major traumas, that undermine the relationship. When one partner sees the other as making demands that are unreasonable or controlling, then his own sense of control is undermined—a primary stress trigger.

Another challenge in daily life stems from the possibility that SDR individuals often interpret everyday exchanges as stressful and threatening. This can occur because of a hostile attribution bias—imagining barbed innuendos in a casual exchange—or because brain wiring has developed around insecure early attachments, leaving a person always on the lookout for difficulties or signs of rejection. Based on these fears, some may also try to restore a sense of personal control by placing unreasonable demands on a partner, such as demanding apologies for fantasy slights or trying to place limits on the time a partner spends with friends and acquaintances. The first step to take in alleviating the tension that will arise as a result of this dynamic is simply to realize that the source of the problem may be biological; though this doesn't make it any easier to come up against, it does mean that it is not based on malice. This can take some of the personal sting out of harsh interactions.

A partner, too, can help manage the stress response by identifying the pattern of behavior—if someone is more likely to withdraw or have a temperamental flare-up—and discussing this when the person is not in the grip of stress. It is possible to slow a person down as she is ramping up, calmly trying to guide her back to a more peaceful state by, for example, helping to come up with a constructive solution to the problem or asking her to go for a walk. Admittedly, it's not easy to play this role time and again and there is not a guaranteed fix, but these are worthwhile ways to approach the problem if it seems someone you love suffers with SDR.

Helping Adults with Stress Dysregulation: What Works?

Fortunately, there are now a number of approaches to dealing with SDR in adults that have been shown to be effective—not only in behavior change but also in actual changes in the brain and in stress physiology, as a recent summary by Bruce McEwen's group indicates. They reflect much of what we have seen all along in our look at how SDR develops and how it works. Each of them is helpful for individuals with SDR, who can look for ways to implement them, as well as for their loved ones who would like to support them— and, each of them is a good way to deal with stress, even when SDR is not a factor.

- *Regular physical activity:* This provides a host of direct benefits to many stress-related physical difficulties—obesity, diabetes, metabolic disorders—but also in increased functioning of the prefrontal cortex (enhancing judgment and executive functions) and the hippocampus (which has many roles, especially in learning). There is also increasing evidence that this may play a protective role in delaying the onset of late-life dementia, including Alzheimer's.

- *Mindfulness-based stress reduction:* In addition to the decreases in anxiety and stress reactivity that we've seen a number of times already, this also reduces the volume of the amygdala, the source of emotional reactions like fear and threat.

- *Social support and integration:* There is ample evidence that the importance of social connections for health becomes even more important as adults grow older. Along with physical activity, this increases prefrontal cortex functioning and strongly supports general health. An important component of this for adults is the opportunity to see themselves as contributors to a purpose beyond themselves, from which they derive a sense of meaning and social integration that is another support for continuing health.

To Work

There is, as might be expected, quite a bit of overlap between the patterns of SDR in relationships and work. The same people with high stress responses that can come across as energetic or alluring in a relationship can also seem hard-charging or passionately committed in work. These traits—shaping the amped-up style that is just what some careers and workplaces demand—can even lead to great success. But it often means that coworkers, and especially subordinates, have to endure highly stressful environments. And it may not work in the long run for the hard-charger if the excess cortisol eventually has its way. A pattern of hypercompetitiveness, suspicion of the motives of colleagues or subordinates, approaching every negotiation in terms of dominance relations, can in some circumstances support a climb toward positions of influence and leadership. This is changing in many modern work settings, which now value collaboration, civility, and teamwork, though the more traditional corporate model of status retains a strong hold. But this hard-charging leadership approach, which can be rooted in SDR, will likely exert considerable costs to health and well-being in the long term. And in the intermediate term, it can lead to career problems as well, as coworkers and superiors tire of walking on eggshells. (But also recall the distinction between teens who are reactively aggressive versus those who are instrumentally aggressive. Adults who use aggression instrumentally as a tool or tactic often are not stress-dysregulated; they are able to self-regulate and often exhibit aggressive displays at little emotional cost to themselves.)

For those who are lower on the totem pole, the work environment can be taxing for another reason, one referred to as the "demand-control curve." This term is used to depict increasing demands on middle managers and lower-level employees and the diminishing control they have in meeting those demands. If, for example, a corporate decision is made at the executive level that costs have to come down, the message is passed on to department managers to create savings at some fixed percentage. They then devise a strategy that is passed along to the middle managers in their units. Until this point in the hierarchy, the demands may be high, but the control is also quite high, typically through the opportunity to delegate. Middle managers, however, begin to feel the pinch, as productivity demands remain high but the resources to meet them are diminished—or diminishing. For them, the demand-control curve begins to rise. The workers who need to maintain the same productivity with fewer colleagues—or perhaps uncompensated overtime—can end up at the very stressful end of this curve. (This can exist in personal life too: if the real or perceived demands of family life heavily outweigh control, our stress response system can be called on far too often, in far too many ways—schedules, finances, child care, and so on.)

On a personal level, the same methods of handling stress in a partner also apply to an SDR boss—or coworker or employee—but, frankly, given the hierarchical nature of these relationships, they can be trickier to put into use. If constructive change is not possible, it's a good idea to seek another work situation, as it is difficult to contribute in a valuable way under these circumstances—for obvious reasons but also because stress, acting as if it were an infectious disease, has the power to spread.

The increasing levels of stress create another complication that has been studied recently as "workplace civility." Many of the uncivil behaviors are clear manifestations of excess stress and SDR: short tempers, "bossy" rather than respectful behaviors, social exclusion of some coworkers. This incivility can spread, and reach levels that carry major costs for the enterprise. A recent *Harvard Business Review* report cataloged many of these costs:

- 48 percent intentionally decreased their work effort.
- 47 percent intentionally decreased the time spent at work.
- 38 percent intentionally decreased the quality of their work.
- 80 percent lost work time worrying about the incident.
- 63 percent lost work time avoiding the offender.
- 66 percent said that their performance declined.
- 78 percent said that their commitment to the organization declined.

Finding ways to address the stress epidemic and SDR in the workplace would clearly have benefits beyond better health and well-being among a firm's employees. It would also likely lead to significant increases in productivity.

STRESS CONTAGION

One of the more surprising findings recently in the research on the stress response system is that stress is, in fact, physiologically contagious. We all know that if a conflict or tension is brewing, it's hard for groups to get things done. What's new in the research is that this is showing up in our underlying biology as well: the stress response becomes attuned across all members of the group. A growing number of studies looking at infants, children, and adults show that when one person generates a strong stress response, others begin to have a similar reaction. Recall the still-face experiment, in which mothers were instructed to do nothing with their faces for a brief period while interacting with their babies. The infants grew visibly distressed rather quickly, and both mothers and babies showed a rise in cortisol levels. This interpersonal synchrony of the stress response has also been observed in other studies of parents with adolescents as they engaged in relaxed versus difficult conversations with each other. Here, what was most interesting about the findings was not so much that both parties became stressed during the difficult exchange—they were, after all, instructed to speak about a recent argument they had had—but more than that, in measuring cortisol in the participants afterwards, they both reached similarly high levels, which illustrates the subtle mirroring that can happen in stress contagion.

Additionally, in studies of adults working in groups—in which physiological stress measures are taken before and after doing a task together—it has been found that a few distressed individuals can lead to similar mirroring responses, what we might think of as team distress. In this case, nothing unusually difficult is introduced, as with the conversation about a recent argument between parents and their kids; simply the presence of stressed individuals can cause contagion. This phenomenon has been tracked with performance outcomes on challenging tasks as well: when the stress synchrony is at a moderate level—indicating joint engagement and purpose in the challenge—performance increases. But when the stress response moves to more elevated levels, team performance suffers.

This isn't a magical process, of course. We've known for some time that our emotional expression is designed by evolution to signal what we've perceived and are responding to. We're wired to make use of that information for survival. We've also known for some time that fear and anger in large crowds can spread very quickly and become hard to control. What this new research is telling us, however, is that this feeling can carry right down to the stress response system, creating a measurable difference in us physiologically.

And the contagion of stress among people who are close to one another—in families or in work settings—means that there is a higher level of ambient stress all around. Many parents bring home the amplified stress they absorb from the outside world, whether that comes from the high-anxiety atmosphere of a job or the economic and domestic pressures of a two-income household. Distressed parents convey their agitation in many subtle and not so subtle ways to their kids and partners. And the feeling can linger for hours, even after the person who carried in the discomfort is no longer there or conflict has been settled.

This spawns a vicious cycle in that higher stress levels in households cause a higher rate of stress methylation in the fetuses of pregnant mothers as well as infants in the developmentally critical period of the first year of life. This contributes to a largely underappreciated aspect of the stress epidemic: there is a much stronger chance of methylating the stress genes of the youngest members of our families, thereby increasing the burden in the overall population. Think of it this way: a bad enough boss, one who causes a physiological stress reaction in his employees, can impact not just his colleagues but their offspring, and *their* offspring for generations to come.

THE STRESS EPIDEMIC

It may not come as a surprise, then, that there has recently been a significant uptick in the numbers of people experiencing the harmful consequences of excess stress. The American Psychological Association has been tracking self-reported stress and health problems since the mid-1990s and notes a significant upward trend in both. More than half of respondents report conditions that are, with high frequency, stress-related.

What has been missing from the discussion so far, however, is an understanding of the hidden biology of stress—specifically, stress methylation and SDR—that is making this epidemic so powerful and creating a spiraling dynamic. There is an increase in the number of people highly susceptible to aggravation because of their amped-up stress response systems. This, in turn, creates ever higher rates of stress methylation throughout the population by making social and interpersonal environments harsher and more unpredictable.

The consequences of our stress epidemic are also apparent in our overall physical health. As this epidemic continues to grow, so too does the number of stress-related diseases and conditions affecting the American people. The Centers for Disease Control and Prevention report an increase in the percentage of adults in the United States who are overweight or obese, from about 55 percent to nearly 70 percent over the last two and a half decades. There are also similar rises in metabolic diseases, especially diabetes. In fact, in just a single decade beginning in 2000, CDC data show that many stress-related health problems increased significantly—the percent rises included the rate of self-reported poor or fair health, up 11 percent; diabetes, up 40 percent; heart disease, up 10 percent; high blood pressure, up 12 percent; obesity, up 13 percent; and the number of self-reported "frequent mental distress" days, up 20 percent. The trend toward sharp increases in stress-related diseases and disorders is unmistakable.

In addition, sleep disorders and sleep insufficiency are also a growing problem. From 1984 to 2012, the proportion of adults averaging less than six hours of sleep per night increased by 31 percent. Recently, the National Academy of Medicine assembled all the evidence linking sleep deprivation to other major diseases. It's a long list, which includes high blood pressure, diabetes, depression, obesity, and even cancer, not to mention early death. A similar list is connected to increases in addiction as well. A recent prominent study by Anne Case and Angus Deaton revealed that the increase in longevity among adults in the United States has reversed itself over the last ten years, specifically among less-educated, middle-aged, white men and women, with the likely cause being heightened substance abuse, as well as suicides linked to depression. Not all of these health concerns arise from SDR, of course, but it is clearly a substantial contributor.

Permeating all these stressors is the downward socioeconomic slide, both real and perceived, which has grown dramatically in our society. So in addition to the daily pressures of the workplace and home, there is a constant, underlying fear that things could go wrong pretty quickly. What looks like a solid lifestyle could evaporate in the blink of an eye—as happened to many families in the Great Recession that began in 2008.

In Chapter 6, I will explore the ways in which a variety of factors—income, assets, education, and family background, among others—influence stress levels and overall health. This is what CIFAR refers to broadly as "social inequality," a heretofore unseen but critical component of the current stress epidemic.

Some Resources for the Stress-Dysregulated Adult

Daniel J. Siegel, *Mindsight: The New Science of Personal Transformation*, Bantam, 2011.

Cedar R. Koons and Marsha M. Linehan, *The Mindfulness Solution for Intense Emotions*, New Harbinger, 2016.

Jeffrey Brantley and Jon Kabat-Zinn, *Calming Your Anxious Mind: How Mindfulness and Compassion Can Free You from Anxiety, Fear, and Panic*, New Harbinger, 2007.

Jon Kabat-Zinn, *Mindfulness for Beginners: Reclaiming the Present Moment—and Your Life*, Sounds True, 2012.

Carolyn Daitch and Lissah Lorberbaum, *The Road to Calm Workbook: Life-Changing Tools to Stop Runaway Emotions*, W. W. Norton, 2016.

Martina Carroll-Garrison, *Let's Get Civil in the Workplace*, Workplace Civility Matters, 2016.

6

THE STRESS EPIDEMIC:

The Hidden Costs of Social Inequality

WE'VE SEEN HOW OUT-OF-CONTROL STRESS ripples through the course of a lifetime, starting with difficulty learning and forming attachments in childhood through a host of psychological and physical maladies in adulthood. This story of individual tragedy, of individual children and their parents attempting to confront a stress system that puts them at a disadvantage in virtually every walk of life, is just the tip of the iceberg in many ways. Our story does not end there, because the stress epidemic has a societal source that keeps propelling it forward: social inequality. There is a shocking array of data showing the extensive and accelerating costs of social inequality that we ignore at our peril. But just as in the case of SDR in individuals, there are remedies that allow us to push back against inequality. We'll take those up in Chapter 7, but the first step is understanding the central dynamics of social inequality and how it wreaks the damage we see all around us.

There is a term in science called "consilience," which is used to describe how two separate explanations—different sets of facts from different approaches—can, when fit together in the right way, suddenly create a much larger picture. One of the best examples comes from the study of evolution. Researchers have followed carefully the ways that fruit fly genes mutate under different conditions that mimic natural selection. Using quite different tools, the study of where fossils are located in geological strata (rocks) provides the evidence for how species change over long periods of time. These two very different sets of superficially unrelated facts—from molecular biology and paleontology—make perfect sense together in support of evolutionary theory: they show how gene mutation leads to changes in organisms over time, though at vastly different time scales. Or consider, the Barker study discussed in Chapter 1, which looked at both characteristics of the placenta and patterns of heart disease in adults. Again, these seem superficially unrelated—from the different disciplines of perinatology and longitudinal epidemiology—but when linked together, they provided the impetus for the study of the developmental origins of health and disease.

And this is what happened for us at CIFAR when we pulled together what we'd learned about stress methylation with epidemiological research about the lifelong effects of socioeconomic status—of being relatively poor or rich—on health. Recall from Chapter 1 Michael Marmot's Whitehall study. It provided us with one of our early clues that something as yet undiscovered was making people in lower socioeconomic circumstances have poorer health than those on a higher perch. Lower-ranking British civil servants were four times as likely to suffer heart disease, chronic lung problems, depression, and earlier death than higher-level administrators. Next, we saw the study by the epidemiologist David Barker revealing that fetal environment could play a role in determining adult health. Finally, there was the study that followed the lives of 17,000 people born in England, Scotland, and Wales over the course of a single week in 1958. My colleagues found that among this group, those with poor socioeconomic standing at the time of birth suffered a wide range of difficulties *throughout* their lives: lack of success in school, delinquency, and low career achievement, as well as mental and physical health problems. This study helped us to understand that there were differences between people on each rung of the socioeconomic ladder, meaning that even at the high end where you might be comparing someone who was rich with someone who was merely upper-middleclass, there was a notable difference in outcomes.

What to make of these findings? Clearly it wasn't simply the difference between people who could all afford adequate nutrition or healthy housing; for people in Britain who had arrived in the middle class, these material resources were universally available, as was access to health care in the UK. There appeared to be a mysterious *x* factor that was taking hold early on and causing an array of problems in all the respondents' lives, ranging from low career achievement to cardiovascular disease. This *x* factor had to be physiological—something that could get under the skin—in order to affect physical health many decades later. It made sense that the way in which people respond to stress, as we discovered, was becoming embedded biologically, because there was mounting evidence that excess stress produced the precise patterns we were seeing in the population. This pointed us like an arrow toward stress methylation, which alters how the genes of fetuses and infants function without changing the basic genetic structure. And this was playing out in a number of destructive ways over the course of our lifetimes.

Consilience continued for us as we looked at epidemiological studies—first within the United States and then in other countries—that built on this revelation. We had the individual mechanism—the biologically embedded stress response—that allowed us to understand the stress epidemic. But now we wanted to identify *the specific societal processes that were causing stress to be so extreme in our society*. So we had a new mystery to solve, this time not at the individual level but at a societal level. We took on the ambitious goal of "diagnosing" society in terms of its prevention or promotion of excess stress and stress-related diseases and disorders.

We started with the strongest set of facts at the population level that we and many others had identified: social inequality, which is *always* related to virtually all health and development outcomes. We also confirmed that the shape of this social inequality was like a ladder: at each rung up or down the socioeconomic ladder, the chances for good health and development outcomes go up or down in the same way. For shorthand, we used the term "social gradient" to describe this ladder of social inequality, because each rung leads you higher or lower on these crucial outcomes. As we've seen, these are not perfect correlations: the evidence for resilience shows that early adversity can be overcome; and stress can happen to anyone at any rung on the ladder, enough to lead to stress methylation and SDR.

But we were still left searching for yet another *x* factor—this time in society—that was generating these population patterns. We started with a couple of basic questions. Do some societies have more inequality than other societies? Do societies change in how much inequality they exhibit? And if the answer is yes to both of these questions, what else could we learn about the factors that contribute to these differences in social inequality?

I've been using the term *social* inequality, rather than just inequality, for a specific reason. Many people think of inequality as interchangeable with income inequality. When you hear of concerns about rising inequality, what most likely comes to mind are changes in how much more unequal incomes have become in recent years—the 99 percent versus the 1 percent, for example. And we were very interested in income inequality as well, but from a slightly different angle. We wanted to know, in comparing countries to each other, how much this income inequality contributed to social inequality—that is, how steep the ladder is from the bottom to the top on outcomes of health and development.

When we compare countries to each other, income inequality is related to social inequality, but it accounts for less than half of the SES differences in health and development. Another important aspect about income inequality is that it doesn't pick up on other parts of SES that are related to the ladder of social inequality. While income captures the amount of money a family is bringing in through earnings and wages, it ignores their general wealth, that is, such things as inherited money, parental safety nets at difficult times, and real estate holdings. These differences in wealth—rather than income—explain a good portion of decreasing social mobility across generations. This results from whether you have a good buffering or safety net. People from wealthier families can protect against a range of economic shocks, from loss of job to unexpected health costs, compared to families closer to the financial edge, even if the latter earn good salaries at a given time. Without that safety net, the wrong shock at the wrong time can send things spiraling downward. The loss of a high-paying job can lead to inability to pay a mortgage, the disruption of having to leave your house, paralyzing depression, and, as we've seen, SDR in children under the age of one. And it doesn't actually have to happen in order to have the effect of raising stress at a critical time, during pregnancy or during the baby's first year. Simply worrying about how badly off we'd be *if* any of those things were to happen can raise stress to dangerous levels. These worries are made worse if you live in a society with high social inequality: the fear of falling is greater if it's easier to slide down many rungs of the ladder.

So we measured inequality using additional factors, important among them parents' educational level and parents' career status. These two measures served as a reasonable proxy for early adversity or early protection against risk. And it is relatively easy to get measures of these. But there are other very important factors, like geography and housing—think of the impact of lead paint or lead-contaminated soil in a number of inner cities—that contribute to social inequality as well. We learned from the work of others that these housing and neighborhood effects have a significant impact on health and development outcomes—and they are correlated with the SES ladder as well.

Studies also show clearly that racial and ethnic discrimination are directly related to social inequality in developmental health outcomes, over and above an individual's socioeconomic status. This inequality, rooted in group membership rather than individual social inequality—based on ethnicity, culture, religion, or gender—is also a contributor to amped-up stress response systems, and potentially to differential stress methylation, although specific evidence on that is not yet substantial. It's easy to see why this would be the case. Think of the African American parents of a baby boy who are concerned not only about how to help him succeed, but merely to survive. The systemic risks for African American children and teens— especially boys—in many U.S. cities are well documented, for example, as in a recent federal study of policing in my hometown of Baltimore, in neighborhoods just like the one where I met Jason. Because these group-based aspects of social inequality don't easily fit into a single measure of SES, they are more difficult to model at a population level. But it is clear that they play a major role in elevated stress responses, and likely in stress methylation.

In experiments that showed acted-out scenes comparing neutral, implicit, and blatant discrimination to participants in the study, African American youth showed an increased stress response to the discrimination episodes, both in cortisol levels and changes in heart rate. This elevated response is not always due to SDR—even though the risk of acquiring that is higher due to high stress among parents in such circumstances—because we depend on our stress system to activate during threatening episodes: this is what being on the receiving end of discrimination clearly is. But the health consequences of excess cortisol across a lifetime are the same whether it comes from SDR or from needing to be constantly vigilant against very real threats. In a number of population studies over the past two decades, African Americans show higher rates of stress-related diseases and disorders, even after SES has been taken into account. One promising note from these experiments, though, is that a strong sense of racial or ethnic identity is an important protective factor against an excess stress response when confronted with discrimination.

As we continued to plot our findings about social inequality based on the social status of one's family—looking at parents' education, career, and income as the measures of SES—we confirmed our earlier findings. Charted on a graph showing the effect of SES on any health or development outcome, the ladder (or gradient) always showed up. There is never a point where the effect of social inequality levels off entirely, which would result in a continuous flat line above some threshold—like the poverty line or being above average on income.

We also saw that it applied to the full range of developmental health problems, as we looked at more and more outcomes: long-term mental and physical health, educational and career achievement, and cognitive and social competence. No matter what component we isolated—whether it was income or career achievement—we found the same ladder. What was most fascinating about this was that it didn't matter if a person had transcended his family of origin's socioeconomic status in his own lifetime—attaining a better education or greater career success or higher income than his parents—*he was more likely to struggle with the range of health issues connected to the social position of the family he was born into.* Simply put, if you are born well off, you have better outcomes. These findings in the world of social sciences are so widespread that they have come to be seen as fundamental facts.

As we dug deeper into our study of social inequality—viewing it through the lens of epidemiology—we realized that its consequences paralleled those of stress. That is, stress cut across all classes, affecting everyone in terms of health. For sure, the risk of early life adversity or stress goes down a bit with each rung up the ladder, but we did not find any level—even at the very top of the socioeconomic range, up there with Bill Gates and Warren Buffet—where there is full immunity from SDR and possible stress methylation. Stress is stress, although it may arrive in different guises at different levels of SES.

We were able to see that this ladder-like gradient pattern—with no clear cutoffs—exists at all levels of SES by zooming in on specific groups at the top or the bottom. Recall that in the Whitehall study, the top-level civil servants fared better than the group of executives just below them. And a similar close-up look at the low end of SES showed that there were rungs of social inequality even within poverty groups. Our CIFAR colleague, developmental psychologist and child policy expert at Columbia University, Jeanne Brooks-Gunn, compared children growing up in deep poverty, those just below the poverty line, and those slightly above that; each step up was associated with better outcomes in developmental health. Imagine that you had a magnifying glass, and could get an enlarged picture of this ladder at any point on it. What you would see—and what we saw—is that there are rungs within rungs, which suggested to us that social inequality was a powerful phenomenon.

In the lowest range of the socioeconomic scale—at the bottom of the ladder—this finding felt so instinctually true as to be obvious. If your parents have very little money or education or career achievement, they're going to be stressed-out just trying to get by; at this level, people are often fighting just to get by. Children in this group were clearly likely to experience a broad range of difficulties with the developmental health issues we were looking at. But why should this also be true throughout the classes—through the middle class, the upper class, and sometimes even up to the top 1 percent?

Why would families making, say, $300,000 a year—or even $750,000 a year—still show signs of stress that could lead to poorer developmental health in their children? Our theory: they're not worrying about their survival, but they are worried about maintaining their status, their children's futures, and where they are going to land if there is a misstep. And striving to maintain that status and their children's prospects can be a source of worry itself: how to manage dual careers along with child-rearing, how to get their children into competitive schools (or even preschools). While it is true that lower SES individuals report that they frequently experience high levels of stress (58 percent in a recent Pew survey), it is also true that substantial proportions of the middle class (37 percent) and even the upper class (29 percent) also report experiencing high stress frequently.

A bit further down the ladder, let's imagine a couple making $150,000 a year in combined income. Perhaps they are worrying about trying to buy a home or losing the home that they bought with all the money they had in savings. Different people have different stressors.

One of the stressors that cuts across virtually all social classes is the pressure of time, described in detail by Heather Boushey in her recent book, *Finding Time: The Economics of Work-Life*

Conflict. Increasing demands to be constantly available to the workplace—from unpredictable shift schedules for hourly workers to the expectation of 24/7 access among professionals and managers—affect the vast majority of parents. Especially for parents of infants, these stressors are accentuated by the absence of family-supporting policies that are found in most other wealthy countries—a topic we'll come back to when we consider how to break this stress cycle where it starts.

The key takeaway here for anyone interested in reducing the stress epidemic is that social inequality is directly implicated in fostering stress generation not only for adults in their daily lives but in how that stress can get under the skin of their children though the biological embedding via stress methylation. Further, the larger the social inequality—that is, the steeper the ladder—the greater the fear, because the potential consequences of falling fast and far down the ladder are that much more significant. "Helicopter parents" didn't arise from nothing; they are enacting the fear, in a high stress way, of loss of status for their children. It doesn't matter if the stressors are different, or even if they occur to a lesser degree; they can all generate the negative impacts of social inequality. The fear and worry also grows in the society as the road to social mobility is blocked, as numerous recent studies in the United States attest.

And this realization of the impact of social inequality occurs with greater consequence and across a wider swath of our population than ever before. If once, in our early history, tigers were the hunters that triggered our stress reactions, steep social inequality is the predator that has so many of us living with dread today.

THE STEEPEST LADDER: INEQUALITY AROUND THE WORLD

Once we'd identified this portrait of social inequality and found a way to reliably measure it, we wanted to learn whether there was a link between social inequality and the occurrence of stress epidemics in some places but not in others. And the best way for us to understand this was to compare levels of social inequality and health and development outcomes in various countries. Imagine, for example, that the social inequality ladder is like a thermometer—when it is particularly steep, the mercury in the thermometer is high; metaphorically, the society is running a fever. We were interested in seeing whether steep social inequality, like a fever, was leading to more problems in the affected populations. And we were also interested in whether, over time, raising or lowering the fever would improve or harm the overall population outcomes in developmental health.

This focus on comparing levels of social inequality across countries, as it turned out, would prove crucially important, not just to better our understanding of this phenomenon throughout the world but because it drove home the point that rising inequality and its biological burdens *are not inevitable*. We came to see that across the range of outcomes in health and development—physical health, mental health, crime, academic achievement, social competence, and participation—lower-inequality nations do much better overall than high-inequality ones. Although all societies show some degree of social inequality, they are far from identical—and the ones that are faring worse, such as the United States, provide a glimpse of the policies that promote and sustain the steepest social inequality and the highest stress environments.

Before turning to the details of those comparisons, it's important to emphasize that these comparisons involved Western, industrialized countries with relatively comparable levels of overall wealth. Stark social inequality, of course, exacts a terrible price in the global South and other impoverished parts of the world. In those cases, though, the problem is extreme scarcity of basic resources, like water or food, with enormous numbers of people impacted. Often this is because a small group at the top acquires and hoards virtually all the national wealth— oil, diamonds, or other natural resources. This leads to drastic health costs in those societies. Simply put, if we look at all countries around the world, the wealthier the country, the better the health of the population in general.

Until, that is, you reach the top level of national wealth, basically the countries we looked at for our comparisons— Germany, Australia, the UK, Norway, France, and Italy, to name a few. The populations of these countries have, for the most part, access to basic survival needs like food and housing. They differ on other dimensions, especially how steep the social inequality ladder is, as we'll see in more detail below.

To measure and compare social inequality in these countries, in one study we focused on measures of adolescent health and development. By adolescence, clear differences have begun to show up on many areas, from academic achievement to self-reported health (how healthy do you feel?; have you had these symptoms in the last month?), reflecting the cumulative impacts of early life stress and how they have played out so far. And we could look at a group whose exposure to different levels of social inequality could be associated with measured *differences* in social inequality—sort of like canaries in a coal mine: they show the effects sooner.

There was another factor that made this study of particular interest: the timing. It covered a period from 1984 to 2009, during which many countries, led by the United States and Great Britain, dramatically shifted their approach to the economy. In particular, the countries began to emphasize the market and privatization while cutting spending on social welfare supports. This approach, commonly referred to as neoliberalism, was perhaps best summarized by Britain's prime minister, Margaret Thatcher, who declared: "Too many people have been given to understand that if they have a problem, it's the government's job to cope with it. . . . They're casting their problem on society. And, you know, there is no such thing as society." This approach, in perhaps softer form, came to be a central narrative for many wealthy countries, not only the UK and the United States. In the United States, this story of overly generous social programs—the "nanny state"—that rewarded working the system over hard work, became the basis for a switch from "welfare" to "workfare" during the Clinton administration. The stories we tell ourselves as a nation have a profound impact on social policy decisions, often even more strongly than empirical findings—a theme we will take up in more detail later.

This shift toward the marketplace as the source of solutions, with a diminished or even vanishing role for the government in social support and protection, posed an interesting question: how would the countries who dropped this safety net most abruptly fare in terms of social inequality in developmental health outcomes?

For this time frame we compared a number of countries in terms of the education, physical health, and social participation of their adolescents. For education, we looked at two groups of adolescents: one set born in 1985, prior to many of the market-based and privatization changes; and a second set born in 1994, after these changes had become firmly established in many of these countries. We then studied self-reported health data among eleven- to fifteen-year-olds in the same countries, at about the same time as the educational achievement assessments. And lastly, we were able to use a composite measure of inequality put together by the United Nations, tapping material inequality, educational inequality, and health inequality. Collectively, these studies allowed us to capture both national average performance—with regard to education and health—and each country's social inequality on those outcomes. In other words, we could take the social inequality "temperature" of a number of equally wealthy countries during the same period of changes in social policy.

What we found was that social inequality tended to be quite similar across the many features of health and development that we and others have examined. This means that if a country had significant inequality in any one area, it would probably also have it in others. And those countries with high inequality typically showed *overall* lower educational achievement among adolescents (measured on an international test) and lower self-reported health in an international survey. Consistently, in other words, we found that the steeper the ladder—as in the United States, the UK, Australia, Canada, and a few others—the lower the overall educational performance and health. Conversely, the less-steep ladder was associated with better educational performance and health. This group included the Scandinavian countries and a number of European countries, including France and Switzerland, among others. The countries with high social inequality and lower overall performance (which we called "low resilience" because their overall health and development fared worse during this era) are compared with the reverse ("high resilience") in Table 1.

TABLE 1: Comparison of Resilience in Countries with Greater or Lesser Social Inequality

LOW INEQUALITY, HIGH RESILIENCE	HIGH INEQUALITY, LOW RESILIENCE
Austria	Australia
Belgium	Canada
Denmark	Ireland
Finland	Netherlands
France	New Zealand
Germany	United Kingdom
Italy	United States
Norway	
Portugal	
Sweden	
Spain	
Switzerland	

These patterns were not entirely surprising to us, because they fit a more general pattern shown in most research on social inequality. For example, in countries with a sharp gradient—a steep ladder—the average mortality rates are worse; on the whole, people will die younger. As shown in Figure 1, the mortality rate per 100,000 adults (ages thirty to seventy-four) for low, middle, and high SES for the United States, Norway, and Sweden. The rate is substantially worse for individuals in the low SES group in all countries, but relatively much worse in the United States. In fact, we can see in the graph below that the average Swede has a chance of dying that is roughly the

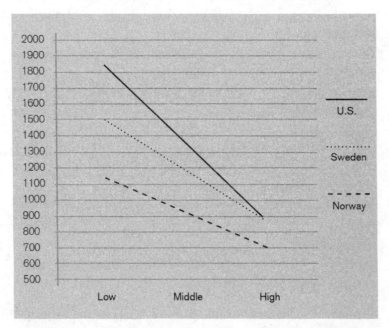

FIGURE 1: Mortality Rates (per 100,000 people from age 30–74) in Three Countries, at Different Levels of SES

same as a U.S. adult at a higher SES level, about the 67th percentile. From looking at the graph, we can also see that the steepness of inequality is highest in the United States. And as we have seen before, this is associated with overall poorer outcomes: the average mortality rate in the whole U.S. population is about 35 percent higher than in Sweden. So, steep inequality has a major impact, even on how long you live, on average.

WHAT LEADS TO SOCIAL INEQUALITY?

It was clear to us, then, that high inequality brought with it steep societal costs. But what in particular was causing the differences between our high- and low-resilient countries? We suspected that income inequality, and the amount spent on social investments like education, were the cause, but we wanted to take a closer look. There was another factor, total national wealth, that we didn't expect to be related, based on previous research. If a specific factor mattered, we would expect that changes in that would lead to changes in the developmental health outcomes of the adolescents. So we tracked how well they did at two points in time about fifteen years apart. This allowed us to look not only at the changes in their overall developmental health and the social inequality—how steep the ladder was—but also the changes in society over that same time period.

When we turned to income inequality—that is, how total national wealth was distributed across different groups in the society—we found that in countries where income inequality had grown rapidly under neoliberalism there was a decrease in overall developmental health among adolescents, and an increase in social inequality. Income inequality did not explain all these differences, but it was a significant factor. Countries with steep ladders had adolescents with worse outcomes.

Another factor that we could measure across countries was the level of investment in human development. Did countries that spent more of their overall wealth on social services, including programs like early childhood education, public education, or training people for second careers have better health and development outcomes? The answer was a clear yes. Countries that lowered their social expenditures—which we can think of as investments in human development—showed decreases in overall adolescent developmental health and increases in social inequality. These programs didn't just make a difference; they made a substantial difference: the higher this investment, the lower the social inequality and the better off the adolescents were in terms of achievement and health.

These findings mirrored other studies on the potential effects of steep social inequality beyond adolescence. Imagine that you're on the way out of your thirty-year job. Not only will you be financially strapped, with few prospects for new employment, but much of your sense of self and personal worth will take a nosedive. Indeed, this seems to be a significant part of the stress epidemic in the United States as it is evidenced in increased mortality among the middle-aged, white working-class people, especially men—reversing a long-standing trend toward increasing longevity.

By contrast, in many of the countries with lower income inequality and higher investment in human development, the picture is quite different. Unemployment is less stigmatized, and the social safety net is more generous, including supports for retraining to enter a new career. These countries tend to follow a model my CIFAR colleague Peter Hall calls "coordinated market economies," in which there is systematic engagement of political and labor leaders with business leaders to establish such supports. And as just noted above, there are no meaningful differences in total economic growth between these two models, the one that is more "coordinated" and the other that is more market-oriented, or "neoliberal." The economies of these countries do go up and down at different time points, but over the decades since World War II the average growth in overall wealth is quite similar. This evidence contradicts a standard argument in favor of tolerating income and social inequality, which is that it is a necessary cost of having strong economic growth.

Put another way, it looks as though the countries with better developmental health and lower social inequality enjoy a better balance between a culture of competition and a culture of care, whereas the countries with poorer outcomes tilt toward an economic philosophy of "everyone in their own boat." Given that economic growth is about the same, the difference can't be easily justified as a tradeoff between economic growth and social inequality.

But then, why would these differences persist? Perhaps it just isn't widely known that social inequality differs so much from country to country, or that it has such a negative effect on how well the population is faring. Because there are many complex data sources to draw from, it's possible that the pattern is not as clear-cut as I've described—although I can say that we didn't go cherry-picking for the data that worked in favor of this view. Many of these are public databases, and more keep coming on line that allow us to look more closely at long-term follow-ups of individuals.

Looking at the consistency that we saw in these patterns, though, we began to suspect that there may be a third factor that determines social inequality, what we at CIFAR came to think of as "the stories we tell ourselves." There are certain countries that have instilled in their citizens an expectation that they will be cared for when the chips are down—as opposed to having to fiercely compete with each other for their basic needs. Indeed, they come to see it as a virtual right of citizenship. A few years ago, the French government announced plans to reduce funding for preschool education, which is available universally. This met with such massive street protests that the proposal was quickly withdrawn. Taking care of young children in these settings was seen as a social obligation and a right of citizenship.

The influence and characteristics of these stories we tell ourselves are difficult to measure. In one of our studies, we did this by comparing two countries that are very similar in many respects: the United States and Canada. Both countries tend toward the higher end of social inequality overall, but with some important differences. Over the same period of time as our study of adolescents, we looked at mortality rates between the two countries and found that the same factors as the ones we found above seemed to matter. Income inequality increased more in the United States, especially when various equalizing factors, like unemployment insurance and health care provision, were taken into account. In both countries, there has been a steady decline in mortality. But this decline in mortality stalled in the United States during this same period, compared to Canada, where mortality continued to drop at about the same pace as previously. And even more recently, the adult mortality rate among white, lower-SES Americans is increasing, as we saw earlier.

We also looked at the impact of national narratives by analyzing the language used in national elections in the two countries. This doesn't perfectly reflect how everyday citizens view their countries, but the electoral stories do need to connect with that. In Canada, for example, even the most conservative parties accepted and acknowledged universal health care as a fundamental right. In the United States, in contrast, much of the political discussion was around reining in social safety net spending, which was portrayed as far too generous. Ronald Reagan's use of the phrase "welfare queens driving Cadillacs" during his unsuccessful 1976 run for the presidency is a memorable example; it became a stand-in phrase for "unfairly living off the system" through the 1980s and into the 1990s, ultimately leading to the dismantling of the existing system of welfare under Clinton and its replacement with "workfare." The "welfare queen" meme appears to have originated with an isolated case that led to a criminal conviction, but that didn't matter: it reflected the view that people should get moving to take care of themselves, rather than "taking" from the government.

It is easy to imagine, though harder to prove, that these messages become part of how individuals think about themselves and their future prospects. In the countries with the highest rates of both social inequality and income inequality, the United States often being the highest among them, the feeling of being left to one's own devices to keep life stable and running at all times is both pervasive and scary as hell when things get tough. The road from there to stress is a pretty straight line.

Which brings us back to stress. I hope it has become clear how the absence of a safety net can set off a vicious cycle. It starts with a new predator—social inequality—that raises stress levels across the board. This elevated stress response can get under the skin of the youngest members of the society, via stress methylation and SDR, either prenatally or in the first year of life. In turn, this raises the total stress that is circulating in the society; more people are stressed-out and carry the burden of SDR, increasing the chances for stress contagion. And around and around it goes, ramping up to what we can clearly see is a growing stress epidemic, with all the health consequences that entails.

So in addition to the important work that we need to do to prevent the development of SDR in early life, and to help children, teens, and adults with SDR cope with that burden, we need to look closely at what we can do at a societal level to ease the burden of SDR. This doesn't mean making society responsible for everything. Individual effort is always a key, but there are things to be done that make that task easier.

7

INEQUALITY IS NOT DESTINY:

How We Can Break the Cycle

THE DISCOVERY OF STRESS METHYLATION has allowed us to pinpoint how and when stress can become embedded in our bodies, and in turn what individuals and their parents can do to avoid it in the first place and deal with it after it occurs. This puts us in a good position to create simpler, better targeted, and more elegant policies that will have an effect at the societal level. We'll now take a look at the big picture because this is where we can organize primary prevention. If we can reduce social inequality—and therefore decrease early life adversity, helping to head off the stress methylation cycle before it gets started—this will have a dramatic impact on people's ability to learn, grow up, and have healthy and productive lives.

CHANGING THE SOCIAL ATMOSPHERE

Since social inequality launches such a vicious cycle, our central goal should be to improve the overall quality of the social environment: make it less harsh and unpredictable. We have the unique potential now to ground social policy in firmer terrain, one that takes into account the biological, developmental, and social aspects that contribute to our overall health and productivity. Translating that potential into reality is an ongoing struggle, one that has its ups and downs, driven by strong economic and political forces. But a clear sense of direction is always an important asset.

INCOME INEQUALITY

Although income inequality and social inequality are not one and the same, income inequality *is* a significant contributor to social inequality. The SES ladder, as I've been calling the graph that charts social inequality—more formally, the social gradient—is far steeper in countries with higher income inequality. Changing this, however, is not an easy task: leveling income inequality, or even altering it slightly, has long been a stubborn challenge, and particularly so over the last thirty-five years.

One measure of income inequality is the percentage of total national income captured by households in the top 10 percent. From 1955 to 1982, this remained quite stable, at just around 35 percent of total income, plus or minus a few percentage points. It began a steady and then accelerating climb, hitting 40 percent of all income by 1986, then 45 percent in by 1996, and 50 percent by 2006—so that by then, 10 percent of households got 50 percent of all income. The same trend shows up when looking at it in another way, such as focusing on the top

1 percent of earners—who garnished 23 percent of all income in 2012 as compared to less than 50 percent earned by the bottom 90 percent of the population.

Reversing this trend would be extremely valuable. Countries with less unequal economic distributions decrease social inequality across the board. But it seems unrealistic to imagine major equalizing shifts in income distribution in the immediate future. History suggests, as do politics, that this will be a long, uphill climb.

And yet, even subtle changes help. There are certain kinds of income redistribution that we often take for granted—and these changes do make a difference. One is a progressive tax system: those with higher incomes pay taxes at a higher tax rate. Taxes and tax rates are a perennial point of political debate, and loopholes and deductions make the taxation system much less progressive than the top tax bracket suggests. But a progressive tax system can shuffle some wealth from higher earners to lower earners and also subsidize, to some extent, the social safety net that limits damage during tough economic times. In the United States, modest changes toward a more progressive taxation system enacted in 2013 have begun to halt rising income inequality, and perhaps bend it slightly toward greater equality—though the 2016 election may check or reverse that modest trend toward less income inequality. And, as Peter Hall and his colleagues have shown, over the long haul, greater levels of social coordination of the market economy—which is correlated with lower income inequality—do not lead to lower overall growth in national wealth. The rising tide that lifts all boats is accurate in the marina, but not in the way that actual economies work. In some countries, the yachts rise much faster.

There are less dramatic ways that mitigate income inequality. In the United States, the earned income tax credit (EITC) funnels money to lower income earners through tax credits. In other words, if they meet certain criteria regarding employment and household income, Uncle Sam pays working families instead of the other way around. Economist Greg Duncan of the University of California at Irvine led a study, published in 2014, that followed families who received the EITC. The study found that the tax credit led to better outcomes for the children. Children from birth to age five in low-income families that received an annual boost of $3,000 went on as adults to earn an average of 17 percent more, and work 135 hours more annually, than similar children whose families did not receive the added income. So not only does this benefit help parents, but it advantages the children too, with effects that continue to unfurl deep into their futures.

Other kinds of income transfers can have similarly valuable results. For example, in our study of income inequality in Canada and the United States between 1984 and 2009, our research team looked at two things: what people earned in a year—that is, their "raw" or "market" income; and what they earned after various tax and transfer policies were taken into account. In Canada, despite higher average tax rates, there are more generous unemployment transfers and child tax credits, as well as publicly provided health insurance. So even though the two countries had strikingly similar changes in raw income inequality, the actual income inequality in Canada was reduced by about 10 percent once all the adjustments and benefits were brought into the equation.

The bottom line is this: income redistribution in various forms reduces income inequality and, in turn, has a beneficial effect on reducing social inequality. Politically, it may be better to call it something other than income redistribution. EITC is often justified not on its benefits but because it rewards families where the parents are working hard and yet still bringing in low incomes. Building on and expanding these and similar programs that are not seen primarily as income redistribution, or even as targeting income inequality, may be an easier path to forge and would make an enormous difference.

There is currently much public debate about raising the minimum wage across the country; some argue that this would have a substantial—and direct—impact on reducing income inequality. In a recent economic analysis of several wealthy countries, this appears to be the case—up to a point. When "maximum efficiency" is achieved—a stage that is hard to predict in advance—the higher minimum wage starts to trend in the opposite direction, increasing income inequality, because at that point the lowest-wage workers are increasingly laid off or given part-time work to reduce labor costs. Whatever its other benefits and consequences, this would be a complicated tool to use for the purpose of reducing income inequality.

These policies provide significant benefits, but even if enacted, they would not carry the entire load of improving the quality of the social environment, leading to a wholesale change in social inequality. Therefore, reducing income inequality is but one step in improving overall social development.

INVESTING IN HUMAN DEVELOPMENT

Supporting citizens by allocating national resources toward such programs as early childhood education or income protection for working adults avoids the uproar that tends to occur when discussing direct income or wealth redistribution. And, by our analysis, as well as others, it also pushes the needle emphatically toward social equality.

In 2010, for instance, Nobel Prize–winning economist James Heckman synthesized a wide array of studies regarding the return on investment in high-quality early education. He found that there were a number of benefits conferred that ultimately reduced overall societal expenditures. Children who were provided with good early development and learning programs, as measured by formal criteria like licensure and less formal observational scales, had better self-reported health, required less special education, graduated at higher rates, had increased employment rates, and, by virtue of their being employed, paid more taxes. That's a lot of bang for your buck. How much? Estimates vary from $2 to $7 saved across time for every dollar invested in high-quality, comprehensive, early childhood development programs.

Given that we can actually put a price on this kind of change, it shouldn't be as difficult a sell as it is relying only on benevolent feelings. But investing in early childhood education is not the only way to improve our social development: we need a comprehensive set of programs that will address every stage of life, so we should aim to do more extensive studies, on a larger scale, along the lines of Heckman's work. This would allow us to invest in targeted programs—with solid research proving their effectiveness—for particular ages, or time cycles, all the way through adulthood. Below, we will take a look at some of the most promising, evidence-based investments that are effective at different stages of development.

NATIONAL NARRATIVES

The third category that our research pointed toward in relation to differences in social inequality across countries is harder to quantify than the others but may prove to be equally or even more important. This is the narrative that a group or nation has developed, both to make sense of their complex social world and foster social cohesion. Something leads countries and groups to make the choices they do, and there are compelling reasons to think they make them because of an overarching variable— these choices fit and reflect the story they tell themselves that informs their worldview. The consistency of societal choices over long periods of time—on income inequality, on investment in human development, on social inequality—is a strong clue that just such a hidden variable may be driving those choices. This is what some social historians refer to as "path dependence": once a particular way of looking at the world is ingrained, it becomes very hard to move that system in a different direction.

Our U.S.-Canada comparison study reflected this insight. We found that Canadians view aspects of social support as a right, rather than as public charity, which is more often the way it is seen in the United States. In Canada, for example, there is virtually no political conversation questioning government support for universal health care: it was an assumed right. In the United States, however, the belief that health care is a right is rarely expressed or proposed in the public domain. With the passage of the Affordable Care Act, there has been a slight shift in view toward a more supportive health care system—Medicare for all—but the continuing resistance in some quarters to incorporating this into the national narrative was reflected in the ongoing battle over its establishment and merits.

And though there has been some progress in changing the mind-set of Americans toward more supportive and caring policies, there remains a clear tilt toward more individualistic self-reliance thinking than in Canada or Europe. With Medicare and Social Security, for instance, Americans have fought to keep them, by and large, because they feel they have paid for them—they are social insurance programs, not handouts. These are viewed as rights not so much because they expand the culture of care but because they are payback for hard labor—and the promises of entitlement in a competitive marketplace. This remains an unresolved tension in the United States, and it's not yet clear if we will be able to move further in the direction of a collective sense of support. The younger generation, however, does show a trend in this regard. In a recent survey done by the Pew Foundation, a federal guarantee of health care was favored by 65 percent of the total population and 71 percent of the millennial generation.

Although it is hard to incorporate this omitted variable of a national narrative into economic equations because it is so hard to measure, a quick comparison of narratives helps to illustrate the phenomenon. The introduction of social support programs like Social Security in Roosevelt's New Deal had multiple goals, but a core feature was that nobody wanted to see their grandparents starve. This same impetus was a factor in Johnson's Great Society programs, which aimed to reduce poverty and deprivation more broadly—powerfully illustrated in Michael Harrington's *The Other America,* published in 1962. But this expansion of social support and antipoverty programs ran into strong headwinds from the 1970s through the 1990s, as we saw earlier, with complaints about "free riders" on the welfare system and the belief that these problems could be handled better through private market solutions rather than government programs. A narrative that is only recently gaining traction, as suggested above, is to make use of actual population outcomes in health and development to guide more judicious choices about *investments* in child development. This makes some supporters nervous, because it still uses the language of the marketplace—return on investments, for example—but it does make it legitimate to look at the effects of social inequality. Yet another view noted earlier is to consider these efforts—or some of them anyway, depending on the country—not as relieving deprivation or as human capital investments, but rather as citizenship "rights." This is a national narrative with considerable sway in many of the High Resilient countries shown in Table 1. But even in some of those countries, the national narrative is being challenged on the grounds that it is overly protective and generous. There is now a political battle in France over standard labor contracts that virtually ensure life tenure for those hired into permanent positions. And the growing concerns about refugee immigration in all of these countries will present further challenges to narratives focused on "citizenship rights." The intensity of the 2016 U.S. election was a clear example of how fraught these competing narratives can become.

Clearly, it's important to recognize the basic need for a balance between a culture of care and a culture of competition, and that there is no final, correct answer to this tension. Going overboard in either direction carries substantial risk. Giving too high a priority to market-based solutions runs the risk—and the reality, as we have seen—of runaway income and social inequality. But eliminating the competitive pressure to produce and innovate runs the risk of economic and social stagnation. Just like an individual's stress system, a well-regulated tension between a culture of care and a culture of competition is most likely to yield the individual and societal outcomes most people seek.

How can we strike the proper balance? First, we should acknowledge that not all the consequences of any policy choice can be predicted. Unintended consequences are an inescapable fact of social change. Second, in the United States, we need to think about policy choices that move the national narrative in a direction that moves toward a better balance, and leads to social policy innovation that is more home-grown than imported. A recent collection that exemplifies this is Jacob Hacker and Ann O'Leary's *Shared Responsibility, Shared Risk*. Third, the crucial but perhaps boring answer is that we need to monitor the outcomes of policy choices carefully and regularly. Making evidence-based decisions using this information is the only reliable way forward, even in our somewhat fact-challenged, postmodern world. A strong argument of this book is that monitoring health and development from the prenatal period onward, especially in terms of the social inequality of those outcomes, should be a central feature of evidence-based social policy decisions.

The knowledge of the link between social inequality, how the resulting stress becomes biologically embedded through stress methylation (and in other ways), the lifelong consequences of SDR for the individual, and the growing stress epidemic should motivate us to seek policies that break this cycle without undermining our basic belief in fairness and individual effort.

POLICIES FOR THE SELF: CONTROL, CONNECTION, AND CONSCIOUSNESS

Another way of getting control of the stress epidemic is to seek policy changes designed to increase support for us individually to avoid stress methylation altogether or to learn to cope with SDR in ourselves or our children. Thankfully, what we have learned about the hidden biology of stress, and how it plays out across the different stages of development into adulthood, grants us the ability to think strategically about effective policy changes.

So let's quickly sum up what the story of early adversity, stress methylation, and SDR tell us about what our targets for policy change and intervention should be.

First, our biological stress-response system has a lengthy evolutionary history. It is triggered under conditions that require us to take action in response to threat or biological necessity. But the disruption of the stress-response system can also pose a long-term risk to health: if the release of cortisol—a hormone central to this system—is too much or too frequent, it can become toxic to internal organs. How the stress system is shaped early on—from the time of conception through the first year of childhood—plays the central role in how it will function throughout a person's lifetime. Throughout, the functioning of this system is closely linked to a psychological sense of *control*, especially in circumstances where our perceptions of the demands being made on us exceed our ability to deal with them.

The second biological and developmental system is related to a sense of social *connection*. Close relationships and warm social interactions generate the secretion of the hormone serotonin, which plays a key role in generating positive emotions, and is the target of a major class of antidepressant pharmaceuticals called SSRIs: selective serotonin reuptake inhibitors, such as Prozac. Together with the oxytocin system, the benefits of social connection in controlling excess stress—by counteracting cortisol—are well established.

A third system, which emerges in adolescence and continues into adulthood, includes aspects of perceived purpose, hope, meaning, and identity. This is a uniquely human process, creating a level of *reflective consciousness* that no other animal possesses. The biodevelopmental focus of this activity largely hinges on the prefrontal cortex of the brain, which undergoes substantial development during adolescence, including increased speed of transmission as well as the amount and complexity of connections from the PFC to other brain systems. This creates the opportunity to create a different view of ourselves in the world. Additionally, through practices such as mindfulness and cognitive behavioral therapy, SDR individuals can train themselves to minimize the effects of excess stress.

Not only should we be aware of the ways we can minimize our stress individually; we should also look to this research as a guide in our larger efforts to address social inequality. Let's examine the social interventions that are aimed at the more modest—and yet still imperative—goal of buffering individuals at critical points, such as when stress methylation takes effect or when we become consciously able to alleviate SDR in ourselves.

FROM CONCEPTION THROUGH THE FIRST YEAR

Since we now know that the critical period for stress methylation is from conception to the end of the first year of life, above all else we should devote our attention to target this period of time in shaping policy that would create a more supportive environment for expectant mothers and new families.

One important stress reducer for expectant mothers is access to quality prenatal medical care, which is important in all cases, but especially when the risk of early adversity is high. This allows for effective monitoring of the health of the mother and fetus, with the availability of appropriate interventions when

needed. It can also reduce stress by providing accurate information and recommending stress management techniques.
Health insurance to make good, affordable prenatal care a reality
is central, of course, and although current changes made by
the Affordable Care Act have helped in this regard, it is still far
from universal. The uninsured rate has decreased by about
10 percent (from a little over 22 percent), though this means that
a substantial number of adults remain without health insurance. Although the potential effect of prenatal stress on the developing fetus has not been a traditional focus of practitioners,
new guidelines from the American College of Obstetrics and
Gynecology strongly encourage inclusion of assessment and rec-
ommendations to avoid excess stress, in part because these hidden biological risks are becoming better understood with new
research. But merely knowing that stress reduction is important
is not enough: we need to look at the real-world changes that
may be needed to make this possible.

Beyond prenatal care, reducing workplace stress, if the
mother is employed, is an important component of intervention. Flexible scheduling, for example, goes a long way toward
offering vital support and reducing stress during this period. In
addition, the U.S. Department of Labor strongly recommends
that employers evaluate the physical demands of any particular
job, make necessary accommodations, and make reasonable
changes to employment policies regarding rest or bathroom
breaks that may be needed by a pregnant employee. The need
for such accommodations should not, of course, be used as a reason to terminate employment, even temporarily, as lack of income is a major potential stressor as well.

There are two other accommodations that can be made to avoid increasing stress during this critical developmental period: wage support during maternity leave and job security afterward. The United States remains an outlier on this front: virtually every European country, as well as other Anglophone countries like Canada and Australia, offer substantial parental leave for families with newborns—but not the United States. Fair and flexible parental leave is widely regarded as a basic social right. It is also important for maintaining the health of new parents and their babies, who are still susceptible at this point to stress methylation. Evidence of the positive effects of such policies is overwhelming. A 2013 review of many countries around the world found that the longer and better supported parental leave policies, the lower the rate of maternal depression, with increased breast-feeding and improved child health outcomes. Yet the United States remains the only industrialized nation that does not have nationally mandated parental leave. Regulatory requirements and/or tax incentives to employers could reduce the stress on new parents, and consequently on the long-term health of their infants.

Not only do we need a better policy in place for parental leave; we also need to encourage Americans to make use of such a policy. Even as more fathers are able to take some amount of leave, we find that they rarely do so. When it is available, almost 70 percent of mothers take advantage of the full amount of leave that is offered, compared with just over 10 percent of fathers. The reasons for not taking leave are similar, typically due to concerns about career advancement or implicit expectations by bosses and coworkers. When Yahoo CEO Melissa

Meyer announced her intention to return to work two weeks after her twins were born, we can only imagine the effect on people throughout the culture. Of course, parents' choices are their own, and the CEO of a major tech company has far more and better options for child care than the average worker. But the public announcement of this approach has certainly been seen by many as a signal about what choices should be made by parents who are serious about their careers and their professional obligations.

Partners and others can provide material support, energy, and social interaction to help avoid a stressed-out state in the mother or baby. Since social connection and warmth are fundamental to maintaining a healthy stress system, new fathers need to view paternity leave as a necessary contribution, not just an option.

There will always be new parents who will need more substantial support, whether because of their personal circumstances or their own developmental histories. Home visits by nurses can be one of the most successful interventions for families most at risk. In 2010, David Olds, a pediatrician at the University of Colorado who pioneered just such a program, summarized the many benefits for the developmental health of these infants. The effect was also familywide, with the latest reports from 2015 showing lower substance abuse among the parents and a greater sense of effective parenting among the mothers, less government spending on food stamps and welfare support among these families, and a reduction in behavioral problems in the children through midadolescence.

EARLY CHILDHOOD AND ADOLESCENCE

Even with successful interventions available during this critical period, some children will continue to bear the burden of stress methylation and its consequences. Perhaps there was too much adversity to overcome—a home-visiting intervention wasn't enough to push back the consequences—or perhaps because of an epigenetic inheritance, when infants are simply handed down the methylated version of the stress gene. In any case, mitigating the difficulties of a disrupted stress system can be enacted not only by the parents but also through early child development programs or at school. Once a child leaves the home, even just for periodic intervals, universal, high-quality early childhood programs—which have a high return on investment, as shown in Heckman's analysis and in the work of many other researchers—have the potential to make a very big difference.

Support for the development and deployment of self-regulation has also been effective in decreasing stress levels among children. Learning the basic skills of self-control, as discussed in Chapter 3—such as those that emphasize simple rules like hug yourself, breathe, count to ten—can go a long way toward helping SDR kids manage their magnified emotions and distress. Learning how to recognize and label emotions has also been shown in a number of recent studies to help schoolkids who have difficulties in managing their behavior and emotions, as early steps toward mindfulness. The resources listed at the end of Chapter 3 provide information that parents can use to help in this effort.

Similarly, building relationships with caring teachers can play a crucial role, offering the benefits of social connection and, in some cases, a second chance for the children who were not able to find this at home. Additionally, there is increasing evidence that mindfulness training, in simplified forms, can make a significant impression on children. This array of school-based interventions—teaching self-regulation, extending social connection, and offering mindfulness training—draws on and helps to establish resilience in children, one of the most effective ways to deal with SDR.

For adolescents, as the bottom brain begins agitating for more exploratory and riskier behavior, while the top brain, the PFC, is still catching up, policies and interventions that reduce the health consequences of risky behavior become very important for everyone, but especially for SDR adolescents, who are more likely to react rashly rather than think things through. Helping them to navigate the new challenges that come with greater freedom is essential and requires creative approaches to protection. One highly effective policy example noted earlier is the graduated driver licensing, which limits the kinds of distractions and stressors that novice drivers are subject to and do not yet have the maturity to handle.

Teens dealing with the burden of SDR, in particular, are more prone to behavioral problems, such as addiction, unsafe sexual activity, and reckless risk taking. These can lead to health problems and, in some instances, early death. Helping kids to get through this high-risk period by supporting them in their transition to adult independence is a major goal. One other example of an intervention that has demonstrated effectiveness in supporting adolescents is comprehensive sex education. This finding is instructive: comprehensive sex education—as compared with abstinence-only sex education—cuts the rate of sexually transmitted infections and diseases among adolescents by about half. Adoption of this model is often held back by moral objections, despite its proven benefits to population health, on the grounds that it will encourage adolescents to become more sexually active. It doesn't, as many studies have shown. A recent national study across the United States showed that states emphasizing the strictest abstinence-only sex education had the highest rates of unintended pregnancy, sexually transmitted infection, and sexually transmitted disease. Again, all of these policies and interventions aimed at protecting the health of adolescents while supporting their growing autonomy benefit everyone, but they are especially important for SDR teens, who are more vulnerable to this wide range of health risks.

ADULTHOOD: HELPING OURSELVES, BUT NOT BY OURSELVES ALONE

When we reach adulthood, we possess many of the cognitive and psychological tools that could support the changes we need to make to lessen our own anxiety and distress—or to help others who might be struggling in this way. Learning how to use those tools is rarely easy, though, especially for SDR adults.

As with adolescents, the same combination of strong social connection and conscious mindfulness offer adults the best antidote to pernicious stress. Our capacity for self-knowledge is stronger at this stage; we've come to know ourselves better and, hopefully, the most beneficial ways to adapt our behaviors in order to minimize stress. Bear in mind, too, that strong connections can still create the opportunity for resilience at this stage; friends and romantic partners can still serve as surrogate attachment figures. Creating the opportunity for these steps to happen, minimizing the opportunities for stress to spiral, and in some cases, seeking professional help, are all ways to advance the goal of helping ourselves.

When it comes to how adults, especially SDR adults, experience stress and become stressed-out, we need to look at where much of the stress originates: in the workplace. Earlier, we learned of the volumes of research on the demand-control balance as a pervasive source of workplace stress: when demands are high and our ability to control the situation is meager, the stress response system quickly becomes amped up. This is further magnified by stress contagion across coworkers—and it diminishes performance for the whole team. Because of this, business enterprises and other organizations have a vested interest in seeking solutions: stress-related health problems undermine productivity, and SDR at the team level undermines performance and innovation. The intrusion of these patterns into the workplace generalizes and magnifies these negative effects on performance and productivity.

We also saw how workplaces and business organizations are faced with the issues of the stress epidemic, exacerbated by the need to work with increasing numbers of SDR individuals. How might they approach the complications of high SDR, arising from internal biological effects on individuals, from external pressures in the workplace itself, or often from both sources, which tend to amplify each other?

First, we need to recall the distinction between being stressed-out and productive stress. High productivity requires a certain level of pressure to achieve, so trying to eliminate stress entirely is not only impossible; it's undesirable. Distinguishing creative stress from punishing stress is important but not always easy. The rapid spread of the stress epidemic suggests, though, that we are tending to an imbalance that features damaging stress too frequently.

From the perspective of an enterprise, perhaps the most important thing to keep in mind is that effective collaboration is rapidly becoming the principal competitive advantage for firms in the knowledge economy—because in a knowledge economy, the human resource for innovation and problem solving is paramount. Excess stress, and stress contagion, creates a barrier in making use of that central resource. Keeping teams on track to productivity is among the most central goals. What can be done to advance that goal?

An important step is to be aware of both the stress epidemic and the presence of SDR individuals on collaborative teams. What seems like discord and conflict for no reason may arise instead from hidden biological processes. Of course, this doesn't mean we should ignore it, but a shift in perspective can help us see that a team member behaving badly may not be doing so by choice. A common response to poor team performance based on internal discord is to ramp up the pressure and increase the consequences and fear of failure. This is unlikely to be productive in the short term, and almost certainly not in the long term.

What can help is to balance a culture of care with a culture of competition, even at the company level. Accommodating real human needs and finding ways to create good social connections among team members—in other words, increasing workplace civility—are effective tools that have been seen to work in many circumstances. Higher-level managers, though, need to be on a special lookout for team leaders and middle managers who are themselves burdened by SDR and can become the source of the problem. Successful delegation to others, whether team leaders or followers, doesn't mean file and forget. Being on the alert for signs of the stress epidemic manifesting itself should lead us to figure out what is going wrong, and then find ways to mitigate the situation.

Finally, in addition to building and sustaining productive social connections among team members, the other tool in the arsenal is to develop a sense of meaning and purpose in the task we have. When people don't know the company's goals, or find them hard to understand or even counterproductive, they are likely to find their stress level creeping up. In addition, getting everyone on board in shaping those goals can smooth over many of the rough spots. This helps individuals to be mindfully engaged in the tasks and avoid being distracted by insignificant issues. To do this, though, it helps if the organization is itself mindful, not only in how to mobilize and maximize the skills available in the workforce but also in clearly articulating its own overall direction.

These factors are unlikely to come together by accident. We

need to keep in mind that this will entail a learning curve, and a fairly steep one at that. But a commitment to being a learning organization must now include our understanding of the previously hidden biology that can bring the stress epidemic to work, hampering the high productivity that is the competitive advantage in a knowledge economy.

BREAKING THE CYCLE

Looking back over the story that links the epigenetic change of methylation in how our genes function, to the lifelong impact this can have on developmental health through SDR, to the role played by the new predator of increasing social inequality, we may begin to feel a bit overwhelmed by the seemingly insurmountable challenge this poses. It can seem even more like our inevitable destiny when we recall the other rub to the epigenetics story: this change to the stress gene can be *biologically inherited*. The amped-up stress system that it leads to may not have been caused by excess prenatal stress on the mother or by early life stress that the infant experienced. Instead, the methylated version might have been passed down from one or several generations back.

But if there are so many possible routes to poorly functioning stress systems, why doesn't everyone suffer? There is a real paradox here. We know, as Steven Pinker described in *The Better Angels of Our Nature*, that the long-term trend across human history is toward less conflict, less overall violence, lowered chances of dying from nonnatural causes, and less harsh social environments. This is hard to square with a pandemic of amped-up, dysregulated stress throughout the whole population. And in comparing different countries today, we also found that some have steeper social inequality, to the detriment of their overall health and development. The countries that are more equal enjoy substantially better overall outcomes. Clearly, then, inequality is not destiny.

What we have seen is that although there are no magic bullets, many things can help to break the cycle. Understanding how the vicious cycle works is an essential first step, but so is understanding the ways that we can interrupt the cycle: for our children, for our loved ones, for ourselves, for the communities where we live and the places where we work, and even for our societies. Redirecting entrenched systems is not easy, but over time, many small changes add up, helping to put in place a virtuous cycle that benefits all of us—and can lead to enduring gains for society as a whole.

EPILOGUE

WE HAVE SEEN HOW SOCIAL inequality, early adversity, stress methylation, SDR, and the stress epidemic are locked into a tight dynamic system, a vicious cycle where each misstep amplifies the next in a continuous loop. This strongly entrenched system makes it challenging to create a more virtuous cycle that promotes health and development. But it is far from impossible. We can look at contemporary comparisons to see countries with a healthier balance, lower social inequality, and better population outcomes. Or we can look back in history and see that there has been dramatic progress in human well-being across the millennia.

But this more positive long-term outlook should not foster complacency. Progress is not guaranteed, especially as we face a raft of global challenges that require solutions in short order. We also should understand how hard it will be. The stress epidemic and stress methylation play a central role in the dynamic system we need to change, but they are not the only factors that are operating here. Other kinds of methylation from social epigenetics are being discovered every day, affecting some of the systems we have discussed, like oxytocin or maternal nurturance. What we do see is that social inequality and early adversity push all of them in a problematic direction. Stress methylation is not the only factor, but because it has such a strong and visible thread from the molecular world to lifelong health to the social world, it is an especially informative one.

Pulling this story together is not possible for one person working alone, and a major side to this story is the progress that comes from broad collaboration across widely different disciplines. I have had the benefit of working with and learning from many brilliant scientists whose efforts lie at the heart of this connected story. Some are mentioned in the book; many are not. But I would be remiss not to mention three close colleagues with whom I worked in the formative period of pulling this human development story together, and all passed away too soon. In addition to the keen personal loss, we all had much still to learn from them. Fraser Mustard, the visionary founder of the Canadian Institute for Advanced Research, pulled me into this adventure at the beginning, when my focus was only on the interface of cognitive science and developmental psychology. Robbie Case and Clyde Hertzman worked with me to formulate the goals of our CIFAR program in human development and helped to build it so that we could tackle the big questions.

Beyond the story of this book, we should take on board one further, even bigger implication. Knowing the long reach of social epigenetics, we can see clearly that how we choose to structure our social world entrenches a complex dynamic in human development. We should now understand that our choices drive our futures, not just in society but in our very biology. The profound realization that evolution is not something that happens to us, but rather a force that we are able to direct, should inspire both hope and a little fear. Poor choices can be built into our biology, but better choices can open up new vistas. It is no exaggeration to say that we control our own future, the future of human evolution.

May we choose wisely.

RESEARCH BACKGROUND: A PRIMER

My goal with this book has been to tell the story of how the new science of biological embedding, particularly social epigenetics, transforms our understanding of the interplay between stress and social inequality and its lifetime of consequences for health and well-being. Early life stress and adversity can launch a vicious cycle, for individuals, for populations, for society—and for generations to come

A key theme of this book is that we need to focus on what the scientific evidence across many different fields is telling us, wherever that leads us. Critical readers—in the true sense of that term, the readers who want to know the facts behind the story, who want to cut to the essence—will rightly want to know how strong the science is. A complete analysis of all the science that went into this story would require a companion book. In this brief addendum, though, I aim to provide a condensed guide to key background readings, a primer of sorts that points the interested reader to the research behind the book. It provides references to some of the work carried out by research teams and collaborators I have worked with directly, but also to seminal work by many other researchers that I have drawn on.

First, though, a brief observation on scientific thinking and methodology may help to frame the discussion. The central story line for this book is on stress methylation as it leads to stress dysregulation, the lifetime of consequences arising from that source of biological embedding for individual and population developmental health, its link to social inequality and the large-scale societal implications of that inequality. Throughout the book, I have noted that there are important features of biological embedding beyond this specific epigenetic methylation (of the gene NR3C1 that exerts control over the glucocorticoid feedback loop). These other kinds of biological embedding include the methylation-demethylation of other key genes in response to social and physical exposures (that is, other genes also listen to the environment in early life), other epigenetic mechanisms and related factors that impact on gene expression, as well as the direct programming of brain development through neural sculpting, also known as synaptic pruning.

So why focus primarily on methylation of this stress gene for the central story line? Mainly because it has several features that carry the story in a coherent way. First, it was the focus of the original groundbreaking work at McGill that largely launched the field of social epigenetics, and the accumulating evidence for its similar operation across multiple species is strong. Second, the site of its action is the HPA axis, and we know a great deal about how dysregulation of the stress-response system affects health and development across the lifespan. Third, this pattern of outcomes from stress dysregulation tracks closely with what we have learned about the nature of the social gradient in developmental health, affirming the view that it is a central player in how social inequality gets under the skin. Fourth, the links from micro to macro show a strong consilience—a jumping together of superficially unrelated findings—that raises our confidence in the main conclusion: a powerful dynamic system connects stress methylation to the effects of stress dysregulation across the lifespan, to the social gradient and social inequality, to how societies differ in the way that they deal with social inequality, and returns full circle to promote or inhibit stress methylation in subsequent generations.

Many readers may be more familiar with—and perhaps more comfortable with—a line of scientific argument that focuses much more tightly on each of the constituent elements. And for many kinds of scientific findings and the argument they make, I would agree. Nailing down the details is absolutely essential to bolster our confidence in important findings. But it is not the only kind of robust scientific argument, in my view. Sometimes, it is the consilience of findings from very different fields and levels of analysis that make the best scientific arguments. Consider, for example, two findings from widely disparate research fields: rapid genetic mutations in fruit flies and the location of fossils in geological strata. Although these are from fields that are quite far apart, both sets of findings provide essential support for the fact of evolution. In turn, evolutionary theory helps us to make sense of both sets of findings—and of course many other findings as well.

Another reasonable concern is whether the findings from the still very new field of social epigenetics are sufficiently numerous and convergent to support my claims. I have described this with a metaphor (Keating, 2016c). Imagine a large group of scientists start looking at a new phenomenon. When there is a positive finding, it is like lighting up a single pixel on a large screen. Soon, many pixels begin to light up, but not enough to see the full picture. But gradually, enough of them light up to begin to show reliable and coherent patterns. Surely we want to make sense of those patterns even before every possible pixel is lit. We can have different criteria for when we call "Bingo!" but in this case, the pattern of early life adversity to epigenetic changes to lifelong impacts on developmental health to social inequality is strong enough to identify it now.

What do we mean by strong enough? In addition to the revolutionary scientific research from social epigenetics to population developmental health, there is also a revolution brewing in scientific methodology. Especially in the empirical social sciences, the exclusive reliance on probability testing—"Is this finding not at chance level, at a fixed probability of, say, 5%?"—is under challenge, for a number of very good reasons. A big one is that negative findings can't get published, so there is what is known as a "file drawer effect"—your nonchance finding (beyond the 5% level, that is) may be overmatched by dozens of chance findings on the same question *that didn't get published because they're not statistically significant.*

The emerging line of thinking about this is to move beyond single-study findings based on statistical probability into the realm of Bayesian probability—in simplest terms, using what we reliably know about a phenomenon as the basis against which to test new findings. This has not been widely embraced yet, because so far it doesn't have a simple statistical toolbox like conventional probability tests. But the logic is straightforward. Don't test your finding against simple probability; instead, test it against the cumulative findings in similar studies that set a baseline of existing knowledge. Here, the emerging accumulation of findings of social epigenetic effects from early life adversity is already setting a strong Bayesian baseline, in my view. In addition, the reproducibility of stress methylation results—another challenge to the scientific canon in the news—is quite good, not only across studies but also across species.

There's another, more pragmatic reason not to wait until all the i's have been dotted and the t's crossed: it is too important for us and for our society. There is a standard that is used in clinical trials of new drugs or other medical interventions that requires the announcement of findings that have a major health impact even before the all the possible research data are in. Although not a clinical trial, the research on early life stress, its biological mechanisms, and its impacts on individual lives and society, meets that standard. The negative social and population impacts from the biological embedding of social inequality are so strong, and avoidable, that we need to take advantage of our best available knowledge, without delay.

A PRIMER

One of the challenges in writing this book has been to bring together many different areas of scientific research, across vastly different levels from basic biological mechanisms to comparisons of societies. To help readers navigate, this research background is organized thematically. Citations in the sections below are included in the references at the end, and that list also includes other relevant studies that are not specifically discussed, for those who would like to explore particular issues in more depth.

The thematic organization begins with a summary of the complex dynamic system that links core biological mechanisms to society and population differences, then moves to a consideration of biological embedding, with a focus on social epigenetics; the impacts of this on stress dysregulation, focusing on how it plays out in individual lives as well as on society and the stress epidemic; how inequality, in the form of the social gradient, is affected by these factors, leading full circle back to how inequality creates the conditions for further stress methylation.

THE BIOLOGICAL EMBEDDING OF INEQUALITY: A COMPLEX DYNAMIC SYSTEM

In Chapter 1, I described the process by which the interdisciplinary group I led at CIFAR identified the complex dynamic system that connects core biological mechanisms to social inequality. The central link is that patterns of early life adversity and stress become biologically embedded in the individual; this then has lifelong consequences for development and health. One measure of adversity is economic and social disadvantage—low SES—but adversity and stress can come in many forms.

The signature of a dynamic system is the existence of a feedback loop that keeps the system in place. In this case, the biological embedding leads to the reproduction of early life stress in the next generation, indirectly through difficulties in nurturing owing to stress reactivity of the parents, or directly, through maternal stress during pregnancy and/or direct inheritance of a methylated stress gene. The connected description of this full story is reflected in two collective volumes (Keating & Hertzman, 1999; Keating, 2011a), and I have summarized the main points in more condensed descriptions (Keating, 2009, 2011b). An early paper in this sequence (Keating & Hertzman, 1999) describes this dynamic system as "modernity's paradox": given the material abundance of wealthy modern societies, why do we continue to see sharply limited life options, and shortened lives, among such a substantial portion of society? The earlier versions focused on neural sculpting as a likely pathway, but they did not include epigenetic mechanisms, which were not on the scene at that point.

EPIGENETICS AND SOCIAL EPIGENETICS

A key scientific link in this dynamic system was the introduction of social epigenetics by Michael Meaney, based on the work of his group at McGill University in Montreal on how adverse rearing conditions in rodents affected the functioning of the stress response system (manifested in HPA axis function) through methylation in a glucocorticoid receptor gene (NR3C1). This initial work appeared soon after (Weaver et al., 2004) and has spawned an exponentially growing body of work that now includes work not only on animals but also on humans.

It is important to note that epigenetic models, like many breakthrough findings, have come under fire for overgeneralization and for downplaying other key factors (Birney et al., 2016). And indeed, there is a risk of interpreting all health and disease processes using the new tools and concepts, overlooking tried-and-true scientific methods. In particular, much of the overhyped interpretations have failed to sufficiently take into account how epigenetic mechanisms relate to other important factors, especially transcription factors in gene functioning. They have glossed over the potentially important distinction among cell types (are the tests done on blood, on saliva, on brain cells?), which has an impact on the causal sequence being unraveled. Study designs have not carefully distinguished between epigenetic changes as the *cause* of disease versus those changes that may possibly have occurred as a *result* of the disease process itself. And finally, reliable evidence that epigenetic modifications can be passed down across generations is limited to three or so generations, and human evidence is particularly limited—which is, of course, in part a function of the length of generations in humans compared to, say, rodents. These are serious concerns, but even the critics see a promising future for the broad field of epigenetics as these concerns work their way into ongoing and future research. (See, for example, John Greally's blog post of July 3, 2016, "The Bright Future of 'Epigenetics'" at http://epgntxeinstein.tumblr.com/.)

The story in this book is of course not about epigenetics writ large but instead focuses on a specific stress gene and the impact of epigenetic modifications to it through DNA methylation. This narrower focus avoids some (but not all) of the emerging critiques just noted. This is not to say that we now know everything we need to know about even this specific biological (and social) process but rather that there is a substantial accumulation of evidence regarding its role. So why choose this specific epigenetic modification?

- Partly as a function of being the first focus of study for the new approach of social epigenetics, the accumulation of key findings in many studies has generated systematic reviews that confirm the main story line (Curley & Champagne, 2015; Kundakovic & Champagne, 2015; Palma-Gudiel et al., 2015; Turecki & Meaney, 2016; Zhang et al., 2015). And as I noted in a recent commentary (Keating, 2016c), evidence of effects on child development from multiple contexts is beginning to appear. This accumulating evidence shows high consistency on key issues: the effect is found in multiple species, from rodents to humans; the effect is nearly always in one direction—early life adversity is associated with stress dysregulation; and the effect has been found using multiple cell types (blood, saliva, and neuronal).
- The focus is on a specific locus of DNA methylation, rather than arising from an epigenome-wide search for all possible effects. But it is also the case that there are multiple epigenetic effects that follow the same pattern of disruption arising from early life (including prenatal) adversity, including later maternal nurturing, impacts on oxytonergic and serotonergic systems, and a wide range of health and developmental outcomes, among

others (see, for example, Babenko et al., 2015; Barua &
Junaid, 2015; Braithwaite et al., 2015; Dettmer &
Suomi, 2014; Lester et al., 2016; Monk et al., 2012;
Provencal & Binder, 2015).

- The specific biological outcome of this epigenetic
  methylation is a dysregulated stress system, and the
  consequences of that "getting under the skin" are well
  known and conform to established social epidemiological patterns in the population—more on both of these
  below.

- One of the most controversial of the claims about
  epigenetic modifications, including DNA methylation, is
  that they are heritable—that is, they can be passed down
  from generation to generation. One of the reasons that it
  is highly controversial is that it throws a wrench into the
  decades-long modern synthesis in evolutionary biology
  that united Darwinian natural selection and Mendelian
  molecular genetics by arguing that acquired characteristics can be inherited, not just genetic mutations
  (Jablonka & Lamm, 2012). This Lamarckian view had
  been seen as discredited, so its emergence in a new way
  is potentially quite disruptive—although integrating
  this inheritance mechanism into a new and expanded
  synthesis seems entirely plausible (Jablonka & Lamb,
  2015). Setting aside the question of how major a role, if
  any, epigenetic inheritance may play in evolution more
  generally, the evidence in favor of heritability of some
  epigenetic modifications is accumulating (Carone et al.,
  2010; Gertz et al., 2011; Sen et al., 2015). Most epigene-

tic modifications are erased soon after conception, so establishing how and why some may survive this process is complicated for several reasons (van Otterijk & Michels, 2016). They may be the product of later intra-uterine exposures; they may have resulted, in the maternal line, to changes in the ova of the gestating female fetus; they may reflect differential genetic susceptibility to epigenetic modification. Establishing this definitively would require evidence from at least three or perhaps four or more generations later, which for humans will take quite a long time, given current technologies. On the other hand, the evidence for transgenerational inheritance of stress epigenetics in both animal and human research is accumulating (Bowers & Yehuda, 2015; Crews et al., 2012; Provencal & Binder, 2015; Sen et al., 2015). Epigenetic messaging about the "preferred" setting of the stress response system might well have a special status, given the importance for survival in dangerous environments. It is important to keep in mind, though, that epigenetic messaging is not the only route to transgenerational inheritance, because the intrauterine environment is affected by maternal stress during pregnancy (Babenko et al., 2015; Barua & Junaid, 2015; Bowers & Yehuda; van Otterijk & Michels, 2016), potentially resetting the epigenetic methylation, and a similar process occurs if stress interferes with effective nurturing after birth. Direct transmission of epigenetic modifications across generations remains a hotly disputed topic, but on balance the evidence favors the probability that it does occur. However, as in all complex dynamic systems, any one process does not act alone. In this case, the multiple processes of direct epigenetic inheritance and indirect inheritance through an altered intrauterine environment and/or through stress-disrupted early nurturing all point in the same direction: the reproduction of stress dysregulation across generations.

EARLY LIFE ADVERSITY AND STRESS DYSREGULATION

The evidence that early life adversity and stress exacts a dramatic cost on subsequent health and development—which we called "developmental health" to emphasize the common pathways that lead to these problems—is by now overwhelming, as summarized in several overviews (Keating, 2011a, 2011b, 2009, and works included or cited in these publications). Indeed, this phenomenon has been encoded into a brief questionnaire format, the Adverse Childhood Experiences, in which adults retrospectively report their experience of early life adversity (Felitti, 2009). Scores on this brief instrument have been consistently related to a wide range of diseases and disorders, many of which are known to be related to stress. Although we should always be cautious about interpreting retrospective recall— because it may have been influenced by subsequent factors, such as experienced illness—the overlap with prospective (that is, longitudinal) social epidemiology patterns inspires confidence in the general findings. And the ease of data collection by ACE on a population basis has made it attractive as a feasible measure for widespread applications, such as by the World Health Organization.

Beyond the general association, we do know a great deal about how stress dysregulation affects subsequent developmental health. The Romanian orphans study has provided some of the most dramatic evidence (Gunnar et al., 2001), but the accumulated evidence across multiple contexts reinforces and extends our understanding of its major role (for example, Gunnar, 2016). Stress dysregulation—both elevated and blunted responding, with the latter associated with more severe trauma—has been associated with and implicated in a wide variety of childhood disorders, but it has also been found to contribute to a wide range of adult health problems. The reason for this has been the focus of years of research by Bruce McEwen and his colleagues (McEwen, 1998; McEwen et al., 2016). The central idea is that the stress response system is designed to be adaptive to the environment it finds itself in, with more dangerous or threatening environments generating a greater response. The general term for this is "allostasis"—akin to homeostasis, as in the body's regulation of internal temperature. The difficulty for longterm health arises by the overexertion of the stress response, which McEwen (1998, p. 33) describes as "allostatic load":

Allostatic load can lead to disease over long periods. Types of allostatic load include (1) frequent activation of allostatic systems; (2) failure to shut off allostatic activity after stress; (3) inadequate response of allostatic systems leading to elevated activity of other, normally counter-regulated allostatic systems after stress.

As noted above in the discussion of consilience, what makes this story of stress dysregulation across the lifespan so compelling is how it matches up with the social epidemiology findings on early life adversity being linked to later problems in developmental health.

INEQUALITY AND POPULATION DEVELOPMENTAL HEALTH

The stress response system evolved as a way for animals to be more adaptive to immediate environmental demands, and the operation of the HPA axis in humans is no different. But clearly, we don't face the same survival threats as our long-ago ancestors, so what is creating such high levels of stress dysregulation and increases in stress-related diseases and disorders that amount to a stress epidemic?

In this book, and elsewhere, I have argued that there is strong support for viewing social inequality as a primary driver of stress dysregulation and, in turn, a stress epidemic. The first line of evidence focuses on the social gradient, the ladder showing the empirical association between levels of SES and a wide range of health outcomes—throughout the population, as well as at higher (Marmot et al., 1984) and lower SES levels (Brooks-Gunn et al., in Keating & Hertzman, 1999). There is strong evidence that shows these SES patterns can be traced back to the family of origin, indicating the impact of early life adversity (a detailed argument and review is in Keating, 2009).

If, however, social inequality is truly a population phenomenon, we would predict two other general sets of findings. The first of these is that there should be an association between the level of inequality in population developmental health in a given society, and its overall performance and well-being—an association that has in fact been observed across multiple outcomes (Keating, Siddiqi, and Nguyen, 2013; and review by Keating, 2009). The other prediction is a bit more stringent: we should expect to see that changes in social inequality are associated with changes in factors that are known to contribute to the level of inequality. Although this is difficult to test, because of data availability in the limited number of countries where data are available, we were able to find this change-change pattern among adolescent developmental health and societal patterns across the "neoliberal era" from the mid-1980s to about 2009 (Keating et al., 2013).

We know by now a substantial amount about the mechanisms through which this is translated into later life health problems, as described above, and why we are seeing an increase in stress-related diseases (Brotman et al., 2007). We are also beginning to learn more about differential susceptibility among different groups in society, including women's risk for cardiovascular disease being exhibited differently from men (Vaccarino & Bremner, 2016), or the particular risks for groups who see their social status as a group declining, as in the pattern reported by Case & Deaton (2015) among middle-aged, lower-SES whites in the United States. This psychosocial stress is related to but also distinct from early life adversity, as defined by low SES. It can occur across the population, arising from multiple sources.

This expanded interpretation of the data on social inequality provides the link for seeing the complex dynamic system at work. Specifically, it indicates that increasing social inequality has the effect of increasing the level of stress dysregulation in a population (as evidenced in increases in stress-related diseases). These higher levels of stress dysregulation have the effect of creating a stress cycle in which expectant and new parents can, by virtue of stress contagion, bring external stress into the family (Palumbo et al., 2016), raising the risk of generating new cases of stress-methylated stress dysregulation in the next generation.

BREAKING THE CYCLE

A key goal of this book is to identify the potential responses to the alarming trends identified by the scientific story. This operates at two levels. The first is what can be done individually and within families to prevent, mitigate, work around, or otherwise defuse this vicious cycle. The resources at the end of each of the chapters looking at stress dysregulation from infancy to adulthood describe the evidence-based methods that can help.

At the societal level, this needs to be addressed in multiple ways. The good news is that addressing issues early in development has demonstrated lifelong positive consequences for multiple outcomes, including both health and development (Boyce & Keating, 2004; Keating & Simonton, 2008). As noted in the final chapter of this book, there are multiple social policies that are evidence-based and can be realistically implemented even in the current political climate (for example, Boushey, 2016;

Hacker & O'Leary, 2012). A more challenging but desirable goal would be to make sufficient changes so that the national narrative about *why* such changes are central to societal well-being, so that they may become socially embedded (Keating et al., 2013; Kitayama, 2013). I have also argued (Keating, 2016a, 2016b) that we should consider the kind of society we want not only in terms of how it affects our health and our children's health and development—the primary focus of the evidence and argument in this book—but also in terms of what "rights" individuals have for opportunities to thrive, rather than struggle, in achieving health and well-being. It is important to note, though, that both the utilitarian and the rights framework point in the same direction: improving the quality of our social environment is a central goal for both reasons.

BIBLIOGRAPHY

Babenko, O., Kovalchuck, I., Metz, G. A. S. (2015). Stress-induced perinatal and transgenerational epigenetic programming of brain development and mental health. *Neuroscience and Biobehavioral Reviews, 48,* 70–91. doi:10.1016/j.neubiorev.2014.11.013.

Barua, S., & Junaid, M. A. (2015). Lifestyle, pregnancy and epigenetic effects. *Epigenomics, 7*(1), 85–102. doi:http://dx.doi.org.proxy.lib.umich.edu/10.2217/epi.14.71.

Birney, E., Smith, G. D. & Greally, J. M. (2016). Epigenome-wide association studies and the interpretation of disease-omics. *PLoS Genetics*, e-published: June 23, 2016, http://dx.doi.org/10.1371/journal.pgen.1006105.

Boushey, H. (2016). *Finding Time: The Economics of Work-Life Conflict.* Cambridge: Harvard University Press.

Bowers, M. E., & Yehuda, R. (2016). Intergenerational transmission of stress in humans. *Neuropsychopharmacology, 41*(1):232–244. doi:10.1038/npp.2015.247.

Boyce, W. T., & Keating, D. P. (2004). Should we intervene to improve childhood circumstances? In Y. Ben-Shlomo & D. Kuh (Eds.), *A Life Course Approach to Chronic Disease Epidemiology*. Oxford: Oxford University Press.

Braithwaite, E. C., Kundakovic, M., Ramchandani, P. G., Murphy, S. E., & Champagne, F. A. (2015) Maternal prenatal depressive symptoms predict infant NR3C1 1F and BDNF IV DNA methylation. *Epigenetics, 10*(5), 408–417, doi:10.1080/15592294 .2015.1039221.

Brotman, D. J., Golden, S. H., & Wittstein, I. S. (2007). The cardiovascular toll of stress. *The Lancet, 370*(9592), 1089–1100. doi:http://dx.doi.org/10.1016/S0140-6736(07)61305-1.

Carone, B. R., et al. (2010). Paternally induced transgenerational environmental reprogramming of metabolic gene expression in mammals. *Cell 143*(7), 1084–1096.

Case, A., & Deaton, A. (2015). Rising morbidity and mortality in midlife among white non-Hispanic Americans in the 21st century. *PNAS, 112*(49), 15078–15083. doi:10.1073/pnas.1518393112.

Crews, D., Gillette, R., Scarpino, S. V., Manikkam, M., Savenkova, M. I., & Skinner, M. K. (2012). Epigenetic transgenerational inheritance of altered stress responses. *Proceedings of the National Academy of Sciences of the United States of America, 109*(23), 9143–9148.

Curley, J. P., & Champagne, F. A. (2015). Influence of maternal care on the developing brain: Mechanisms, temporal dynamics and sensitive periods. *Frontiers in Neuroendocrinology, 40*, 52–66. doi:10.1016/j.yfrne.2015.11.001

Dettmer, A. M., & Suomi, S. J. (2014). Nonhuman primate models of neuropsychiatric disorders: Influences of early rearing, genetics, and epigenetics. *Institute for Animal Laboratory Journal, 55*(2), 361–370. doi:10.1093/ilar/ilu025.

Eiland, L., & Romeo, R. D. (2013). Stress and the developing adolescent brain. *Neuroscience, 249,* 162–171. doi:10.1016/j.neurosci-
ence.2012.10.048.

Fareri, D. S., & Tottenham, N. (2016). Effects of early life stress on
amygdala and striatal development. *Developmental Cognitive Neuroscience, 19,* 233–247.

Felitti, V. (2009). Adverse childhood experiences and adult health.
Academic Pediatrics, 9, 131–132.

Gertz, J., et al. (2011). Analysis of DNA methylation in a three-
generation family reveals widespread genetic influence on epigenetic regulation. *PLoS Genetics,* e-published August 11, 2011.
doi:10.1371/journal.pgen.1002228.

Gunnar, M. R. (2016). Early life stress: What is the human chapter of
the mammalian story? *Child Development Perspectives, 10*(3), 178–183.
doi:10.1111/cdep.12182.

Gunnar, M. R., Morison, S. J., Chisholm, K., & Schuder, M. (2001).
Salivary cortisol levels in children adopted from Romanian orphanages. *Developmental Psychopathology, 13*(3), 611–628.

Hacker, J., & O'Leary, A. (2012). *Shared Responsibility, Shared Risk.*
New York: Oxford University Press.

Hanson, J. L., Albert, D., Iselin, A. M. R., Carré, J. M., Dodge,
K. A., & Hariri, A. R. (2015). Cumulative stress in childhood is
associated with blunted reward-related brain activity in adulthood.
Social Cognitive and Affective Neuroscience, 11(3), 405–412.
doi:10.1093/scan/nsv124.

Jablonka, E., & Lamb, M. J. (2015). The inheritance of acquired
epigenetic variations. *International Journal of Epidemiology, 44*(4),
1094–1103.

Jablonka, E., & Lamm, E. (2012). Commentary: The epigenotype—a dynamic network view of development. *International Journal of Epidemiology, 41*(1), 16–20. doi:10.1093/ije/dyr185.

Keating, D. P. (2009). Social interactions in human development: Pathways to health and capabilities. In P. Hall & M. Lamont (Eds.), *Successful Societies: How Institutions and Culture Affect Health*. New York: Cambridge University Press.

Keating, D. P. (Ed.). (2011a). *Nature and Nurture in Early Child Development*. New York: Cambridge University Press.

Keating, D. P. (2011b). Society and early child development: developmental health disparities in the nature-and-nurture paradigm. In D. P. Keating (Ed.), *Nature and Nurture in Early Child Development*, pp. 245–292.

Keating, D. P. (2016a). Social inequality in population developmental health: An equity and justice issue. In S. Horn, M. Ruck, & L. Liben (Eds.): *Equity and Justice in Developmental Science: Theoretical and Methodological Issues,* 75–104. UK: Academic Press.

Keating, D. P. (2016b). The evolving capacities of the child: Neurodevelopment and the children's rights. In M. D. Ruck, M. Petersen-Badali, & M. Freeman (Eds.), *Handbook of Children's Rights: Global and Multidisciplinary Perspectives,* 1–36.

Keating, D. P. (2016c). Transformative role of epigenetics in child development research: Commentary on the special section. *Child Development, 87*(1), 135–142.

Keating, D. P., & Hertzman, C. (Eds.). (1999). *Developmental Health and the Wealth of Nations: Social, Biological, and Educational Dynamics*. New York: Guilford Press.

Keating, D. P., Siddiqi, A., & Nguyen, Q. (2013). Social resilience in the neoliberal era: National differences in population health and development. In P. Hall & M. Lamont (Eds.), *Social Resilience in the Neo-liberal Era*. New York: Cambridge University Press.

Keating, D. P., & Simonton, S. Z. (2008). Developmental health effects of human development policies. In J. House, R. Schoeni, H. Pollack, & G. Kaplan (Eds.), *Making Americans Healthier: Social and Economic Policy as Health Policy*, 61–94. New York: Russell Sage.

Keverne, E. B. (2012). Significance of epigenetics for understanding brain development, brain evolution and behaviour. *Neuroscience 264*, 207–217. doi:10.1016/j.neuroscience.2012.11.030.

Kirby, J. N. (2016). The role of mindfulness and compassion in enhancing nurturing family environments. *Clinical Psychology Science and Practice, 23*(2), 142–157.

Kitayama, S. (2013). Mapping Mindsets. *Observer, 26*(10).

Kundakovic, M., & Champagne, F. A. (2015). Early-life experience, epigenetics, and the developing brain. *Neuropsychopharmacology, 40*(1), 141–153. http://doi.org.proxy.lib.umich.edu/10.1038/npp.2014.140.

Lester, B. M., Conradt, E., & Marsit, C. (2016). Introduction to the special section on epigenetics. *Child Development, 87*(1), 29–37. doi:10.1111/cdev.12489.

Marmot, M. G. (2015). The health gap: The challenge of an unequal world. *The Lancet, 386*(10011), 2442–2444. doi:10.1016/S0140-6736(15)00150-6.

Marmot, M. G., Shipley, M. J., & Rose, G. (1984). Inequalities in death: Specific explanations of a general pattern? *The Lancet, 1*(8384), 1003–1006.

Massey, D. S. (1995). The bell curve: Intelligence and class structure in American life. *American Journal of Sociology, 101*(3), 747–753. doi:10.2307/3121812.

Masten, A. S. (2001). Ordinary magic: Resilience processes in development. *American Psychologist, 56*(3), 227–238. doi:10.1037//0003-066x.56.3.227.

McEwen, B. S. (1998). Stress, adaptation, and disease: Allostasis and allostatic load. *Annals of the New York Academy of Science, 840,* 33–44.

McEwen, B. S., Nasca, C., & Gray, J. D. (2016). Stress effects on neuronal structure: Hippocampus, amygdala, and prefrontal cortex. *Neuropsychopharmacology Reviews, 41,* 3–23. doi:10.1038/npp.2015.171; 19.

McGowan, P. O., Sasaki, A., D'Alessio, A. C., Dymov, S., Labonté, B., Szyf, M., & Meaney, M. J. (2009). Epigenetic regulation of the glucocorticoid receptor in human brain associates with childhood abuse. *Nature Neuroscience, 12*(3), 342–348. http://doi.org.proxy.lib.umich.edu/10.1038/nn.2270.

Meaney, M. J. (2001). Maternal care, gene expression, and the transmission of individual differences in stress reactivity across generations. *Annual Review of Neuroscience, 24,* 1161–1192. doi:10.1146/annurev.neuro.24.1.1161.

Monk, C., Spicer, J., & Champagne, F. A. (2012). Linking prenatal maternal adversity to developmental outcomes in infants: The role of epigenetic pathways. *Development and Psychopathology, 24*(4), 1361–1376. http://doi.org.proxy.lib.umich.edu/10.1017/S0954579412000764.

National Academies of Sciences, Engineering, and Medicine. (2016). *Parenting Matters: Supporting Parents of Children Ages 0–8.* Washington, DC: National Academies Press. doi:10.17226/21868.

National Research Council. (2011). *Explaining Divergent Levels of Longevity in High-Income Countries.* Washington, DC: National Academies Press. doi:10.17226/13089.

Offord, D. R., & Boyle, M. H. (1988). Prevalence of childhood disorder, perceived need for help, family dysfunction and resource allocation for child welfare and children's mental health services in Ontario. *Canadian Journal of Behavioural Science/Revue canadienne des sciences du comportement, 20*(4), 374–388. doi:http://dx.doi.org /10.1037/h0079940.

Palma-Gudiel, H., Córdova-Palomera, A., Eixarch, E., Deuschle, M., & Fañanás, L. (2015). Maternal psychosocial stress during pregnancy alters the epigenetic signature of the glucocorticoid receptor gene promoter in their offspring: A meta-analysis. *Epigenetics, 10*(10), 893–902.

Palumbo, R. V., Marraccini, M. E., Weyandt, L. L., Wilder-Smith, O., McGee, H. A., Liu, S., & Goodwin, M. S. (2016). Interpersonal autonomic physiology: A systematic review of the literature. *Personality and Social Psychology Review.* E-publication in advance. doi:1088868316628405.

Provençal, N., & Binder, E. (2015). The effects of early life stress on the epigenome: From the womb to adulthood and even before. *Experimental Neurology, 268,* 10–20. doi:10.1016/j.expneurol.2014 .09.001.

Sen, A., Heredia, N., Senut, M-C., Land, S., Hollocher, K., Lu, X., Dereski, M. O., & Ruden, D. (2015). Multigenerational epigenetic inheritance in humans: DNA methylation changes associated with maternal exposure to lead can be transmitted to the grandchildren. *Scientific Reports 5,* 14466. doi:10.1038/srep14466.

Sheinkopf, S. J., Righi, G., Marsit, C. J., & Lester, B. M. (2016). Methylation of the glucocorticoid receptor (NR3C1) in placenta is associated with infant cry acoustics. *Frontiers in Behavioral Neuroscience, 10,* 100. http://doi.org.proxy.lib.umich.edu/10.3389 /fnbeh.2016.00100.

Sullivan, M. (2015, March 4). Putting health into context. *Harvard Gazette.* Retrieved from http://news.harvard.edu/.

Trentacosta, C. J., Davis-Kean, P., Mitchell, C., Hyde, L. & Dolinoy, D. (2016). Environmental contaminants and child development. *Child Development Perspectives*. doi:10.1111/cdep.12191.

Turecki, G., & Meaney, M. J. (2016). Effects of the social environment and stress on glucocorticoid receptor gene methylation: A systematic review. *Biological Psychiatry, 79*(2), 87–96.

Vaccarino, V., & Bremner, J. D. (2016). Behavioral, emotional and neurobiological determinants of coronary heart disease risk in women. *Neuroscience and Biobehavioral Reviews*. E-publication in advance. doi.org/10.1016/j.neubiorev.2016.04.023.

van Ijzendoorn, M. H., Bakermans-Kranenburg, M. J., & Ebstein, R. P. (2011). Methylation matters in child development: Toward developmental behavioral epigenetics. *Child Development Perspectives, 5*(4), 305–310.

Van Otterijk, S. D., & Michels, K. B. (2016). Transgenerational epigenetic inheritance in mammals: How good is the evidence? *FASEB Journal, 7,* 2457–2465. doi:10.1096/fj.201500083.

Weaver, I. C., Cervoni, N., Champagne, F. A., D'Alessio, A. C., Sharma, S., Seckl, J. R., et al. (2004). Epigenetic programming by maternal behavior. *Nature Neuroscience, 7,* 847–854.

Weaver, I. C. G., Champagne, F. A., Brown, S. E., Dymov, S., Sharma, S., Meaney, M. J., & Szyf, M. (2005). Reversal of maternal programming of stress responses in adult offspring through methyl supplementation: Altering epigenetic marking later in life. *Journal of Neuroscience, 25*(47), 11045–11054. doi:10.1523/JNEUROSCI .3652-05.2005.

Zhang, T. Y., Labonté, B., Wen, X. L., Turecki, G., & Meaney, M. J. (2013). Epigenetic mechanisms for the early environmental regulation of hippocampal glucocorticoid receptor gene expression in rodents and humans. *Neuropsychopharmacology, 38*(1), 111–123. http://doi.org.proxy.lib.umich.edu/10.1038/npp.2012.149.

Zhou, Z. E., Yan, Y., Che, X. X., & Meier, L. L. (2015). Effect of workplace incivility on end-of-work negative affect: Examining individual and organizational moderators in a daily diary study. *Journal of Occupational Health Psychology, 20*(1), 117–130.

ACKNOWLEDGMENTS

IT MAY BE CONVENTIONAL TO say that this book could not have been written without the support and contributions of many people. For this book, this conventional acknowledgment is true many times over. Drawing as I have on the collaboration and suggestions of many researchers and clinicians across many different disciplines from epigenetics to epidemiology, from developmental and clinical psychology to psychiatry, from political economy to neuroscience, it is no exaggeration to say I could not have done it without their generous contribution in time, thought and energy, from the past to the present. So, thank you: Tom Atkins, Ron Barr, Jane Bertrand, Eileen Bond, Gerard Bouchard, Tom Boyce, Jeanne Brooks-Gunn, Robbie Case, Kristen Chapman, Max Cynader, Ron Dahl, Dana Dolinoy, Greg Duncan, Jim Dunn, Barrie Frost, Megan Gunnar, Peter Hall, Jon Heidorn, Clyde Hertzman, Howard Hu, Ed Huntley, Magdalena Janus, Jenny Jenkins, Deb Kop, Marc Lewis, Dona Matthews, Margaret McCain, Bruce McEwen, Michael Meaney,

Rosanne Menna, Fred Morrison, Fraser Mustard, Chuck Nelson, Keith Oatley, Dan Offord, Nigel Paneth, Charles Pascal, Christine Power, Martin Ruck, Doug Ruden, Sir Michael Rutter, Arjumand Siddiqi, Kelly Michaels Soluk, Kirk Soluk, Larry Steinberg, Steve Suomi, Richard Tremblay, Cesar Valdez, Susan Watts, Doug Willms, Jean Wittenberg, and Anita Zijdemans.

Special thanks to Tim Bartlett and Annabella Hochschild at St. Martin's Press, to Nell Casey, to Katie Olney for manuscript assistance, and to my agent, Susan Rabiner, for their thoughtful editing and support in this venture.

And my most special thanks to Fiona Miller, for psychological and clinical insights too numerous to count, for unfailingly thoughtful input as first and last reader and editor, and for keeping our family humming through the trials and tribulations of this exciting venture.

Finally, given the many different topics I have sought to bring together in this story, it is especially important to note that the errors or omissions that remain are mine alone.

INDEX